UPES NIGRA

RMSWORTH ISLAND

KOREA

SANDY ISLAND

JUAN DE LISBOA

GROUP

TERRA AUSTRALIS INCOGNITA

PHANTOM
ISLANDS

DIRK LIESEMER studied at the Henri-Nannen-Schule in Hamburg and has worked as a newspaper editor in Berlin and Munich. He currently lives in Munich and works as a freelance journalist and author.

Dirk Liesemer

PHANTOM
ISLANDS

Translated by Peter Lewis

First published in Great Britain in 2019 by
HAUS PUBLISHING LTD
4 Cinnamon Row
London SW11 3TW

First published in German in 2016 as
Lexikon der Phantominseln by Dirk Liesemer
Copyright © 2016 mareverlag, Hamburg

The moral rights of the authors have been asserted

Maps by Peter Palm, Berlin

A CIP catalogue record for this book is available from the British Library

ISBN: 978-1-912208-32-6
eISBN: 978-1-912208-33-3

Typeset in Compatil Text by MacGuru Ltd

Printed in the Czech Republic

hauspublishing.com
@HausPublishing

For Andrea

CONTENTS

9 Foreword

12 Antilia
16 Atlantis
20 Aurora Islands

24 Baltia
26 Bermeja
30 Bouvet Group
38 Breasil
42 Buss
46 Byers and Morrell Islands

50 California
56 Crocker Land

62 Devil's Island

66 Frisland

72 Harmsworth Island

80 Juan de Lisboa

84 Kantia
86 Keenan Land

90 Korea

94 Maria Theresa Reef

98 New South Greenland

109 Pepys Island
113 Phélipeaux and
    Pontchartrain

116 Rupes Nigra

120 Saint Brendan's Islands
126 Sandy Island
132 Saxemberg

136 Terra Australis Incognita
140 Thule
144 Tuanaki

146 Willoughby's Land

150 Author's Notes

153 Bibliography

FOREWORD

For many centuries, seafarers, kings, military and naval commanders, pirates and cartographers believed in the existence of islands that were never there in reality. Time and again, expeditions set sail to try to survey them, and more than a few captains reported having actually set foot on Aurora, Breasil, Frisland, Juan de Lisboa, the 'island' of California or the great southern continent of Terra Australis.

The tales of 30 phantom islands contained in this book are 30 journeys across the world's oceans and back and forth through its history. Every island has its own particular story, yet between the lines, the mindset and the perceptions of the period in which each story first was peddled or gained common currency shine through. For example, it was surely no coincidence that geographers began to postulate the existence of a 'magnetic island' just as the first ships' compasses became widespread in Europe. Among the Spanish conquistadors, ideas circulated of a fabled island of gold and a rocky island with sheer cliffs that was home to half-naked Amazons. Devout Christians, meanwhile, dreamt of a Utopia of pious Catholics in the middle of the Atlantic, while at the same time fearing Satanazes, the Devil's Island.

More than a few of these phantom islands had their origins in ancient tales or mythical accounts, for instance Thule or Atlantis, the existence of which was seriously posited even in maps of the early modern period. Other islands derived from reports that were passed down through generations by word of mouth; thus it was that the Irish priest Saint Brendan was said to have gone in search of the Isle of the Blessed. His wanderings are recounted in more than 100 different variations. Yet other islands can be traced back to curious logbook entries, shimmering mirages and simple misunderstandings, or even to subtle jokes, downright deception and reprehensible grandstanding. For each case, we can only speculate exactly how the particular ingredients coalesced into a story and how seafarers might have blended their own experiences with hearsay accounts.

The voyages of discovery that were undertaken in the Age of Exploration introduced errors into the early inventories of geographical knowledge on a grand scale. To begin with, the earliest navigational maps ('portolan charts') contained little more than lists of ports and dangerous reefs. Many a supposition was founded on quirky theories, such as that of the equilibrium of the Earth. This was used, for instance, to support the theoretical presence of great landmasses in the southern hemisphere or in the Arctic Circle around the North Pole. While a number of phantom islands drifted around early maps like rudderless ships, perpetually on the periphery of the known world, others had their rivers, mountains and cities documented by name.

Many islands were places of longing, such as the philosophers' island of Kantia as well as Saint Brendan's Islands or Antilia. This latter island may well, moreover, have facilitated Christopher Columbus's first voyage westward to the New World. And non-existent islands repeatedly became the focus of squabbles between states; England, for example, declared a good dozen of them sovereign royal territory. As a result of its War of Independence, the United States secured the possession of two supposed islands in Lake Superior. The International Date Line was even once given a kink to the west in order to ensure that the day ended on an American phantom island.

Often, the process of refuting the existence of an island is more exciting, but also more complicated and dangerous, than its discovery. There are quite a few Germans in the ranks of the debunkers of phantom islands, for example the aviation pioneer Hugo Eckener, the zoologist Carl Chun and the polar explorer Wilhelm Filchner, who, at the beginning of the 20th century, even risked his life to prove that an island did not exist.

These 30 stories are not just oddities, however. They can also be read as part of a much larger narrative: we humans are forever trying to gain an overview of the world and yet are prey to the provisional nature of all knowledge. We strive for definitive certainty and, in so doing, barely look beyond the horizon of our own age. We forget all too easily that cartographers had to learn from the ground up to distinguish between myths, opinions and facts; it took a long time before a reliable stock of knowledge could be amassed. The precise image of the world as we know it is only a very recent achievement.

Today, pretty much everywhere has been explored, measured and researched. But even now, old discoveries suddenly wash up again like flotsam. Not long ago, Mexican parliamentarians found themselves arguing over the whereabouts of a supposed island in the Gulf of Mexico. Even more recently, in September 2012, press reports emerged about the futile search for a Pacific island that had found its way onto digital maps of the region.

It may well be that there are still dozens – or even hundreds – of phantom islands to be found on navigational charts. After all, Indonesia alone is believed to comprise no fewer than 13,677 separate islands, and possibly more than 17,000. Worldwide, there are estimated to be at least 130,000 islands, possibly as many as 180,000 – surely a broad enough surface on which to project some new tall tales. One of the latest stories only began on 19 February 2000. A newspaper reported that astronauts aboard the US space shuttle *Endeavour* had spotted an unknown archipelago in the Andaman Sea, a marginal sea that forms part of the Indian Ocean. A chain of seven islands was clearly visible there, they claimed, arranged in a rough circle off the coast of Thailand. In the centre was an even larger island, like the pupil in the middle of an eyeball; the whole ensemble had supposedly resembled nothing so much as an elephant's eye. Who knows? Maybe these islands will make it onto a map before it's acknowledged that the astronauts' supposed report was a hoax and that these islands are entirely fictitious too.

ANTILIA · ATLANTIC OCEAN

[ATULLIA, ANTILLIA, ILHA DAS SETE CIDADES]

Position 31st parallel north

Size comparable to Portugal

Sightings 1447

Maps Pizzigano Brothers (1367),
Zuane Pizzigano (1424), Martin Behaim (1492)

IRELAND

ANTILIA

Canary Islands

Cape Verde Islands

GUINEA

Who knows? Had it not been for Antilia, Christopher Columbus might never have ventured as far out over the Atlantic as he did. A long way off in the ocean, so the story went in the 15th century, lay an island by the name of Antilia. Anyone who set sail to try to find a passage to Asia could drop anchor off its shores as a final port of call. There, they could take on board fresh water, fruit, victuals and a whole lot more besides. 'This island has such an overabundance of precious stones and metals that the temples and royal palaces are covered with plaques of gold,' wrote the Florentine astrologer and mathematician Paolo dal Pozzo Toscanelli in a letter of 25 June 1474.

By then, seafarers had been exploring the Atlantic for some time, frequently discovering new islands, such as the Azores and the Canary Islands. But still nobody knew how far to the west the ocean extended. Eventually, it was speculated, you would reach the coasts of Asia – the subject of Marco Polo's famous account – including the wealthy empire of China and the mysterious Japan.

To get to Antilia, Toscanelli's letter explained, all one needed to do was to set sail heading due west from Lisbon and remain on that course. He omitted to say how many days it would take by ship to reach the island, but from there, it was just a short step to Japan – of that he was certain. 'Only another 225 leagues,' he claimed: in other words, barely 1,100 kilometres. The addressee of Toscanelli's letter was Fernando Martinez, the canon of Lisbon and a confidant of the King of Portugal in whose name many voyages of exploration had already been embarked upon. The Florentine scholar also made a copy of the letter to give to his friend, the navigator Columbus. It was for this reason that Columbus was allegedly so sure that a voyage across the Atlantic was a manageable risk, provided he could find his way to Antilia.

Toscanelli was not the first to mention Antilia. The name of this island, or at least a very similar-sounding one, could be found on a map prepared by the Venetian brothers Domenico and Francesco Pizzigano.

Although they didn't actually depict the island, on the far western extremity of their world map, next to the figure of a man with his hand outstretched, is a barely legible legend: 'Here are the statues that stand off the coast of Atullia and which were erected for the protection of seafarers; for beyond is the abominable sea, which sailors cannot navigate.' Presumably, the 'statues' are a reference to the so-called 'Pillars of Hercules' which, according to legend, were intended to warn ships that they were approaching the Mare Tenebrosum ('Sea of Darkness') – the uncharted regions of the western Atlantic.

Several decades later, the brothers' descendant Zuane Pizzigano, likewise a cartographer from Venice, included for the first time an island, shown in bold pillar-box red, on his 1424 portolan map (an early maritime chart) of the Atlantic Ocean. The island, a wide rectangular bar, is situated off the west coast of Portugal, and next to it are the words *ista ixola dixemo antilia*: 'This island is called Antilia.' It appears to be a mirror image of Portugal, and indeed its name derives from the Portuguese *ante-ilha*, which translates into English as 'ante-island' or 'facing island.' The younger Pizzigano's depiction of the island includes seven bays, which take cloverleaf-shaped bites out of its interior. On each of these bays is a city. North of Antilia, a squarish and somewhat smaller island rises out of the sea: a blue island by the name of Satanazes, or Devil's Island (see p. 62).

It is surely no coincidence that Antilia bears a resemblance to Portugal. 'In AD 734, when the whole of the Iberian Peninsula had been conquered by heathens from Africa, Antilia – which also goes by the name of Seven Cities – was occupied by an archbishop from Porto, Portugal together with six other bishops and other Christians, men and women, who had fled there from Spain by ship with their livestock, property and goods,' the Nuremberg cartographer Martin Behaim wrote onto his Erdapfel (literally 'earth apple'), the world's first globe, which he made in 1492. However, he got his dates wrong: the 'heathens from Africa,' that is the Moorish invaders, had taken control of the Iberian Peninsula by 714, not 734.

14

While Behaim was still completing his globe, Columbus weighed anchor and headed west with his fleet of ships. For weeks on end, he sailed in the direction of Asia. Though there are no notes written by the navigator himself to confirm it, Columbus certainly knew about the island of Antilia and may well have assumed that he could make an intermediate stop there. Indeed, it is clear that the existence of the island would have made his pioneering voyage appear far less perilous. In the event, it was only 1,000 kilometres west of the point where Antilia had been charted that Columbus's lookout finally spotted land: the Caribbean archipelago. Columbus christened the group of islands the Antilles.

On maps made after Columbus's return, Antilia shrank in size. Even so, Christians continued to peddle the story; they dreamt of an island of Catholics – a 'Christian Utopia' – where the old observances could be preserved. They even told themselves that a Portuguese ship had reached the island of Antilia in 1447. It was said that the sailors had encountered people there who spoke Portuguese and that the first thing they wanted to know was whether Muslims were still ruling over their homeland of Portugal.

ATLANTIS · ATLANTIC OCEAN

Position north of the Equator
Size comparable to Europe
Sightings uncertain
Maps Athanasius Kircher (1644)

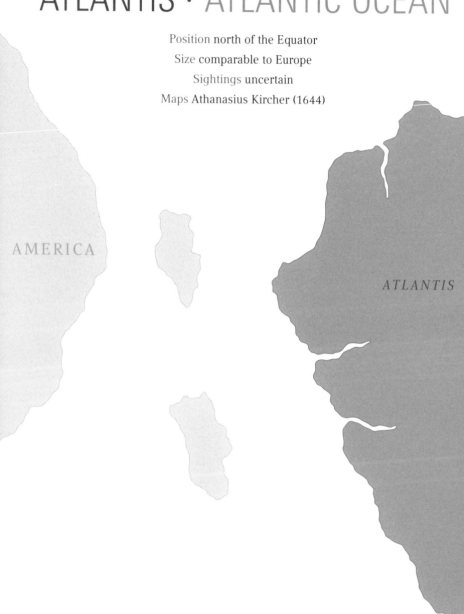

AMERICA

ATLANTIS

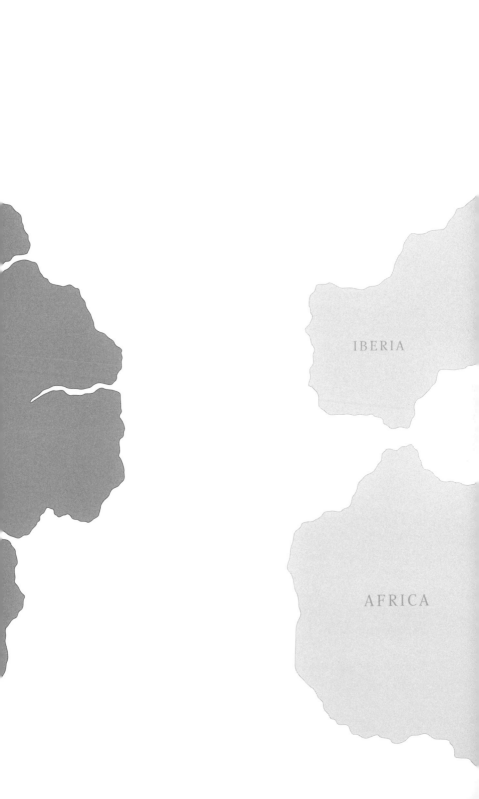

IBERIA

AFRICA

The Earth has a body and a soul. And, like blood in the human body, the ocean currents circulate around the globe. During ebb tides, the water is drawn into the interior of the Earth's body, while at times of flood tide, it is pumped forth once more. The Earth's skeleton, so argued the Jesuit scholar Athanasius Kircher, is made up of the mountain chains that hold the planet together. These ranges extend around the entire globe. In some cases – such as the Alps or the Himalayas – they soar high above the Earth's surface, but then plummet down into the ocean and run across the sea floor. In certain places, the peaks of these seamounts appear above the surface of the water as islands.

In the 17th century, Kircher was counted among the world's greatest polymaths. He taught at the Jesuit Roman College, which would later become the Pontifical Gregorian University, and read the Ancient Greek philosophers in their original language. Kircher also occupied himself with such diverse subjects as volcanoes, Ancient Egypt and whether flying dragons had ever existed. At one point, he even drew a number of sketches in order to work out whether the Tower of Babel might actually have been able to reach the moon.

To test his skeleton theory of the Earth, Kircher decided to study the history of the fabled island of Atlantis. According to Plato, this island sank beneath the waves of the Atlantic Ocean in the space of just a single ill-fated day and night. First it was rocked by an earthquake, and then a tidal wave swept all the land into the sea, taking with it all the people who lived there. This catastrophe was said to have taken place more than seven millennia before Plato's era. The Athenian philosopher wrote about Atlantis in around 360 BC and, in the process, quoted Socrates as having maintained that the subject had the great advantage that it was not some fabricated fairy tale, but instead could be traced back to a true story.

For a long time, scientists assumed that Atlantis was nothing but a myth. This ended, however, with the discovery of the New World – an event that no one in Europe had reckoned with. Where had the people there come from? Might there not once have been other lost worlds on our planet?

Kircher was the first geographer to include Plato's Atlantis on a map. In 1644, he placed the island roughly halfway between North America and the Iberian Peninsula. In this, he was adhering to tradition: according to Plato, Atlantis – which was larger than North Africa – lay far out in the Atlantic, beyond the Pillars of Hercules. On Kircher's map, the outline of Atlantis resembles that of South America as it is shown on the world map in Flemish mapmaker Abraham Ortelius's famous atlas of 1570, *Theatrum Orbis Terrarum* ('Theatre of the World'). But in comparison to South America, Atlantis is significantly smaller and is rotated 180 degrees so that the 'southern' tip in fact points northwards. Alongside the island is a cartouche containing the words *Situs Insulae Atlantidis, a Mari olim absorpte ex mente Egyptiorum et Platonis descriptio*, which can be translated as 'Site of the island of Atlantis in the ocean, from Egyptian sources and Plato's description.'

At the time in which Kircher's map was published, Europeans believed passionately in the existence of the sunken continent. Kircher's statement that he was drawing on Egyptian sources as well as Plato supported the commonly held assumption that the Ancient Egyptians knew more than contemporary people had previously imagined. However, neither here nor in his book *Mundus Subterraneus* ('Subterranean World') did Kircher reveal his exact sources.

It is not beyond the realms of possibility that the Jesuit was simply indulging in a little joke with his reference to Atlantis; it certainly wouldn't have been the only one he played. For instance, Kircher was fond of boasting to his contemporaries that he could read hieroglyphs, though this was long before they were to be deciphered. Nobody ever dared to challenge the eminent scholar on this score.

AURORA ISLANDS
SOUTH ATLANTIC

Position **53° South, 48° West**

Size **118 kilometres long,**
possibly comprising several islands

Sightings **Amerigo Vespucci (1504)**, the *Aurora* **(1762)**,
Alessandro Malaspina (1794), the *Helen Baird* **(1856)**

Maps **Laurie & Whittle (1808)**

30°

SOUTH
AMERICA

40°

50°

Falkland Islands

AURORA ISLANDS

South Georgia

60°   50°   40°

Early in 1504, Amerigo Vespucci set sail from South America. He sailed southeast with the prevailing winds, far out into the cold, rough South Atlantic, which at that time was almost entirely uncharted. The farther south his fleet ventured, the less visible the familiar constellations of the northern hemisphere became, and little by little, they disappeared below the horizon. By 3 April, not even Orion or the Plough (the Big Dipper) could be seen anymore. Vespucci calculated his position as a latitude of 53° South, meaning he must therefore have been in the vicinity of the Falkland Islands, though they were not discovered until 1592.

As if from nowhere, a storm blew up, the wind began to howl and the ships' masts started creaking. 'So violent was the storm that the whole flotilla feared for its safety,' Vespucci noted. Waves crashed over the bows and the sea threw foamy spray across the deck. The commander ordered the sails to be reefed; his ships were 3,000 kilometres from the coast of South America and were drifting straight into the middle of the Antarctic winter. The days grew ever shorter and the nights ever longer: 'The night of 7 April lasted for 15 hours.' Then, all of a sudden, a 'new land' appeared before the sailors' eyes, a 'wild shore' that was not marked on any map. For hours on end, they sailed along the coast of the island in icy weather: 'We sighted not a single harbour nor a single living soul.' The island measured almost 20 leagues – around 110 kilometres – in length. It finally disappeared from view as Vespucci and his crew sailed on without having set foot upon it.

The island remained unknown and uncharted for 350 years. Cartographers speculated that Vespucci might simply have sighted a gigantic iceberg. Alternatively, had he come across a volcanic island that, like Atlantis, had since sunk beneath the waves once more? Or had he just been tricked by some Fata Morgana?

A new sighting of the island was made in 1762. The Spanish merchant ship *Aurora* was sailing from Lima in Peru to Cádiz in southern Spain.

It had rounded Cape Horn and was making its way across the South Atlantic when it reached the same point that Vespucci had given as the location of the island. There, the crew sighted not one but several islands, which in time would come to be named the Aurora Islands after their ship.

Over three decades later, the Spanish survey vessel *Atrevida*, under the command of Alessandro Malaspina, set sail in search of the archipelago. The ship headed due east from the Falkland Islands. On 21 February, at around half past five in the afternoon, the captain noted in his logbook: 'To the north, at some considerable distance, we perceived a dark mass, which seemed to all of us to be an iceberg.' They steered a course towards the apparition and ultimately saw 'a magnificent mountain in the form of a pavilion (or tent), split vertically into two halves: its eastern tip was white, while the one to the west was very dark in colour.' The ship approached to within one nautical mile of the coast. The following day, another island came into view. It was 'likewise covered with snow, though not as high as the first.' On 26 February, a third island was sighted 'which at first appeared to us to be a huge ice floe; however, its complete immobility ultimately persuaded us that it was in fact an island.' All three islands were situated at 53° South, 48° West – roughly halfway between the Falkland Islands and South Georgia.

Thereafter, the Aurora Islands remained unsighted for a long spell. Following a futile voyage in search of them in 1827, the British Antarctic explorer James Weddell speculated that the islands the Spanish sailors had spotted 'might possibly have been the Shag Rocks.' These rocks rise out of the South Atlantic like jagged teeth; they are located at the same latitude as the supposed Aurora Islands, but lie significantly further to the east.

In the meantime, the island group provided the perfect material for fiction. 'On the eighteenth we found ourselves about the station indicated [...] and cruised for three days in that neighborhood without finding any traces of the islands [...] mentioned,' runs the account in *The Narrative of Arthur Gordon Pym of Nantucket*, Edgar Allen Poe's 1838 novel, which immortalised the Aurora Islands in literature. Nonetheless, Poe's fictional hero was searching too far to the southeast, some 1,300 kilometres away from the position indicated by the crew of the *Atrevida*.

By the mid-19th century, the islands had come to be regarded as something of a myth when they suddenly reappeared for one final time. 'The Auroras, covered in snow: two islands in sight (one large and one small),' the captain of the *Helen Baird* recorded on 6 December 1856. His crew made out 'five islands all told.' Who can say how many will appear the next time the island group is sighted?

BALTIA · BALTIC SEA

[BALCIA, BASILIA, BASILEIA]

Position uncertain
Size uncertain
Sightings uncertain
Maps uncertain

How magnificently the Circus Maximus was decked out! Everywhere you looked, there was a sparkling, shining and shimmering golden hue. Never was there more amber in Rome than during the reign of Emperor Nero. Even the draperies around the stadium's imperial podium were decorated with amber, Pliny reported, and the weapons of the gladiators and the stretchers for the corpses had the same magical glow about them. Just recently, a legionary had been said to have dragged a huge block of amber into the Eternal City, weighing no less than 13 pounds!

Rome was enthralled, and the natural historians of antiquity began to speculate on the origins of this precious stone. Some believed that it was obtained from mines in Liguria. Others wondered if it might come from trees that grew on remote, rocky outcrops bordering the Adriatic; some were sure that, whenever the Dog Star appeared in the sky, a resinous sap seeped from the bark of those trees and hardened soon afterwards to produce amber. Others were convinced that it derived from various fossils found in Northern Europe – this explained why amber was sometimes white, while at other times it was waxy coloured, or reddish. Still others believed that it was washed up on the banks of the River Po.

Ultimately, one of the oldest suppositions turned out to be nearest to the truth. As early as the 4th century BC, the Greek geographer Pytheas mentioned an island by the name of Basilia, which was situated in the Baltic Sea (precisely where remained unclear, however). Pytheas made his living as a merchant in Massalia – today the French city of Marseilles – and travelled far and wide throughout Europe. It is thought that he may have sailed through the Strait of Gibraltar, travelled extensively around Britain and even reached Thule (see p. 140), before finally fetching up in the Baltics, where he learned about the existence of Basilia. Pytheas's travel reports have long since been lost – we know of them only as a result of later authors quoting them – and so it remains a matter of dispute as to which island in the Baltics he once identified as Basilia.

Diodorus of Sicily added a number of details to Pytheas's report. Diodorus, who lived during the 1st century BC, changed the name of the island and relocated it to 'above the province of Gallia' where, he claimed, 'there lies in the ocean an island by the name of Basileia. Onto this island the sea casts large quantities of electrum, which is otherwise found nowhere else on the inhabited Earth. Many ancient authors promulgated incredible myths about electrum, which posterity has refuted.' In any event, he claimed, the island's inhabitants transported electrum to the mainland, from where it made its way to Italy and Greece.

As its historic name – electrum – implies, amber does have an electric effect. If you rub it, the Roman writer Pliny the Elder observed in the 1st century, amber attracts chaff, dry leaves and even iron filings; for this reason, amber was long thought to have healing properties. Pliny also noted that ants, gnats and lizards were often found trapped within amber; accordingly, he reasoned, it must once have been in a liquid state. He knew virtually nothing about the island of Basilia, but he did note that it was reputed to lie three days' journey from the coast of the Scythians – a catch-all term for many northern peoples – out in the Baltic Sea. Presumably it did exist, though no one can say now with any certainty to which of the Baltic islands 'Basilia' originally referred.

BERMEJA · GULF OF MEXICO

[VERMEJA]

Position 22° 33' North, 91° 22' West
Size 80 square kilometres
Sightings Alonso de Chaves (1536)
Maps uncertain

The Triangle

Cayos Arcas

BERMEJA

Scorpion Reef

22°

Sandy Island

New Bank

Sisal Bank

MEXICO

After a period of almost 500 years during which there had been no sightings of Bermeja, in the summer of 2008, the Mexican Parliament suddenly began to take an interest in the whereabouts of this island. Before long, suspicions were being voiced that it had been blown up by the CIA. The United States was seeking to gain control over the oil-rich maritime region, it was claimed. And didn't it have a track record of having stolen large tracts of territory from the Mexicans in the aftermath of a war? The country's politicians feared that, if the island had indeed vanished, Mexico's loss of sovereign territory would also mean losing the mining rights to rich petroleum deposits beneath the seabed. The upshot was that a parliamentary commission authorised a large-scale operation to find Bermeja.

Mexico had always been deeply concerned about its sovereign territory. For centuries, the very first description of the Gulf of Mexico was treated as classified information. In 1536, in his work on navigation *Espejo de navegantes* ('Mariners' Mirror'), the Spanish seafarer and cartographer Alonso de Chaves mentioned the island of Bermeja for the first time: 'An island close to the peninsula of Yucatán, it is situated at 23 degrees. It lies 14 kilometres west of the Cape of Saint Anthony.' Chaves further reported that Bermeja was a small island that from a distance appeared to be bright and of a reddish hue.

Thereafter, Bermeja appeared as a small patch of land on maritime charts of the Gulf of Mexico; its coordinates were 22° 33' North, 91° 22' West, and it lay 160 kilometres off the Yucatán Peninsula. In 1775, a Spanish naval squadron under the command of Miguel de Alderete set out to chart the contours of the ocean floor and to glean more information about the islands in the Gulf of Mexico. His logbook recorded the hourly position and bearing of the fleet, the wind direction, the degree of precipitation, the distance covered and the results of the soundings taken, yet this expedition never set eyes on Bermeja. Likewise, British ships plying the waters of the gulf reported no sightings of the island. But even though Bermeja was never sighted again, the island – or had it only ever been a low-lying reef? – did not sink into oblivion.

There is a clear and simple definition of islands in international law. All they are required to be is a land mass that is entirely surrounded by water. The country to which an island belongs also has sovereign rights over the sea within a radius of 200 nautical miles around it. Nonetheless, in a report published in 2009 on the whereabouts of Bermeja, the Mexican geographer Carlos Contreras Servin declared this definition to be insufficient. He was concerned about the 223 reefs of the Sonda de Campeche, which were being increasingly swamped by the rising sea level. As things stood, Mexico could still claim them as sovereign territories, but what would happen when global warming caused the sea level to rise even further? Would Mexico have no choice but to renounce vast possessions in the Gulf of Mexico?

In the summer of 2009, at the behest of a parliamentary commission, the Mexican Air Force conducted an aerial survey of the gulf. In addition, the National Autonomous University of Mexico despatched the research ship *Justo Sierra*; on board was a team of experts from various disciplines, drawn from no fewer than seven universities. Soon after, the Secretariat of the Navy ordered the *Tuxpan* to join the search, followed by the *Kalin Haa*. The vessels found several reefs, such as Scorpion Reef and the Isla de Arena, the existence of which had been doubted for a long time. But there was no sign of Bermeja.

In spite of this, Mexico did not have to renounce its sovereign rights in the Gulf of Mexico. Treaties were concluded with the United States in 1978 and 2000 on territorial demarcation lines in the gulf – greatly to the benefit of the Mexicans. Over and above this, in 2007, the country also successfully lodged a claim with the United Nations to control additional sea areas closer to the United States' territorial waters. These lie much farther out in the gulf from the Mexican coast than Bermeja supposedly did. This concession has finally allowed Bermeja to slip into obscurity.

BOUVET GROUP
ATLANTIC OCEAN

Position 54° 26' South, 3° 24' East
Size 9 kilometres long, 7.5 kilometres wide (Bouvet Island)
Sightings 1739, 1825, 1898
Maps uncertain

*THOMPSON
ISLAND*

B O U V E T   G R O U P

BOUVET & HAY

54°

*LIVERPOOL
ISLAND*

BOUVET ISLAND

LINDSAY ISLAND

4°   5°

On a cloudless Sunday morning, the *Valdivia* left the harbour at Cape Town to sail around the cape. The sun was just rising, its rays flooding over Table Mountain, whose deep gorges were picked out in dark shade against the brightly lit face of the escarpment. The German zoologist Carl Chun stood on deck and gazed wistfully at the receding shore. He had spent seven days in the city with his fellow researchers and had, amongst other things, attended an unforgettable banquet held by the Gesellschaft Germania ('Germania Society'), a German expatriate association, where cabaret artistes performed, speakers vied with one another to win the audience's favour and an oompah band played.

It was 13 October 1898, a few days later, when the white-hulled vessel *Valdivia* slipped her moorings to leave the cape and head out into the Southern Ocean, a place where ships rarely ventured. 'If you look at one of the maritime charts prepared by the British and track across the broad, uncharted expanse of ocean directly south of the Cape of Good Hope, you only come across a single indication of land, and even that is designated as speculative,' wrote Chun. Three islands were thought to be situated in the South Atlantic, just south of the 54th parallel: these formed the Bouvet Group. Several expeditions had already gone in search of them, but in vain. The last sighting had occurred 75 years previously.

In 1739, the French explorer Jean-Baptiste Charles Bouvet de Lozier first sighted an island in this location. He determined its coordinates to be 54° South, 4° 20' East, and believed it to be the foothills of Terra Australis Incognita – the 'Southern Continent.' The island was not sighted again for a long time thereafter: James Cook failed to find it in 1775, as did James Ross in 1843. Nevertheless, in the meantime, two British whalers maintained that they had seen the island: James Lindsay in 1808, and Captain George Norris in 1822. Norris even claimed to have set foot on it. He also sighted another island nearby, which he christened Thompson Island, and declared both to be British sovereign territory. In the interim, however, so many different coordinates had been suggested for the group that it was thought as many as five islands might exist: Bouvet, Bouvet-Hay, Thompson, Lindsay and Liverpool Islands.

The *Valdivia* steamed steadily onwards; the air was clear, and the sea was calm. Chun and Captain Adalbert Krech decided to look for the Bouvet Islands. The *Valdivia* had thus far shown herself to be an excellent ship. She was a refitted steamship of the Hamburg-Amerika Packetfahrt-Actien-Gesellschaft ('The Hamburg–America Packet Shipping Joint-Stock Company' or HAPAG for short). On 31 July 1898, she had set sail from Hamburg on a voyage that would cover 32,000 nautical miles. To begin with, the ship headed north around the British Isles, before turning south and steaming down the west coast of Africa to Cape Town. The *Valdivia* then set off towards Antarctica. Subsequently, she would explore the Indian Ocean, sail through the Suez Canal into the Mediterranean and thence return to her home port. The sheer amount of scientific data ultimately gleaned from this voyage turned out to be immense; it filled 24 volumes, the last of which was only completed in 1940.

In the course of their expedition, the German scientists investigated one last great *terra incognita*: the deep-sea floor. Chun had to lobby for many years to get the expedition off the ground, making formal submissions for funding and holding countless lectures. On hundreds of occasions, he advanced the argument that the English and the Americans had already begun to study the ocean floor and that it was high time Germany got involved in this research. Finally, Chun was appointed leader of the first major German expedition to study the depths of the ocean.

In the late 19th century, the deep sea still exerted a great fascination on people's imaginations. 'At times, people thought it was unfathomable and devoid of all organic life,' wrote Chun, 'while on other occasions, the public saw it as the mirror image of the terrestrial topography of our planet, and peopled it with fantastic creatures.' Ocean floor research began in 1818, when in the course of a voyage to Baffin Bay – which separated northern Canada from Greenland – the British rear admiral John Ross retrieved a living basket star (*Gorgonocephalus* sp.) from a depth of 1,500 metres. It had become caught in the ship's plumb line and was the first piece of tangible evidence that life existed at such extreme depths.

By 14 November 1898, the *Valdivia*'s researchers had already lowered their plumb lines to more than 4,000 metres. On the surface, the waves were riding up past the height of a two-storey house, and the temperature was dropping. At midday it was 17.4°C, but at the same time two days later it would be only 7.8°C, and by 22 November it would go on to fall to -1°C. Even so, those on board the research vessel were enjoying the cold, as many of them had contracted malaria during their stop in South Africa. Nonetheless, the chill arrived so quickly that hardly any of the crew escaped coming down with a cold. Eventually, the steam heating system was switched on, filling the saloon and the cabins with a cosy warmth.

On 20 November, the air pressure suddenly dropped. On board the ship, they could see the sky darkening and growing steadily blacker against the foaming white crests of the towering waves. The wind swung to the south, coming from the direction of the Antarctic and blowing a force 10 gale, powerful enough to uproot trees on land. Waves crashed against the side of the ship, washing over the decks. The *Valdivia* hove to, so as to prevent itself from being swamped. All of a sudden, a penguin appeared in the raging sea. It gave a hoarse cry and flapped frantically with its flippers, leaping above the waves here and there, and followed the ship. Overhead, greyish-white seabirds wheeled around the steamship.

The next morning, the sun broke through the clouds. A swell was coming from the north. The sea was wild and of a glorious blue colour, flecked with white foam. The *Valdivia* was steaming into the wind and the waves slapped incessantly against her sides. In the laboratories, glass beakers toppled off shelves, fluids for preserving specimens trickled down stairways and swivel chairs rolled across the saloon. Plates, knives and spoons rattled in their racks and trays. The stewards sashayed over to tables, carrying trays of breakfast. Nobody envied anyone who 'had at one and the same time to try and keep an eye on a soft-boiled egg and a brimming cup of tea,' reported Chun. Around midday, the barometer rose still further. The wind dropped and swung to the north. The deck was pelted by rain and hailstones. A layer of mist floated above the water, forcing the ship to proceed at only half speed. The foghorn sounded at regular intervals so that its noise might rebound back off any iceberg that happened to be floating in their path.

On 24 November, the expedition reached the 54th parallel, where the British Admiralty charts showed three Bouvet Islands. Now and then, the sun broke through and the clouds dispersed briefly, yet the wind kept blowing as an icy northerly blast, covering the deck with sheet ice. The navigation officer had noted on a map the coordinates of all the sightings of land they had made, and the crew were hopeful of finding the islands. Just a few days earlier, they had still been sounding depths of between 4,000 and 5,000 metres – on two occasions, even more. The day before, though, the seabed had been 3,585 metres beneath them, while it now stood at only 2,268.

The *Valdivia* was evidently sailing over a seamount, which might well have formed the base of the islands. There now ensued a systematic search of the area from east to west. All the while, the air remained curiously hazy, while microscopic algae gave the water a greenish hue. As evening approached, a shaft of sunlight burst through the clouds. The crew gathered on deck; there appeared to be something on the horizon. They strained their eyes and blinked, spellbound... False alarm! It turned out to be nothing but some imposing cloud formations.

The following morning, 25 November, the ship was right in the centre of the region where the island group had supposedly been sighted. However, the ocean depth had grown again – to 3,458 metres. Only the profusion of birds in the sky suggested there might be land nearby. The researchers caught two Namaqua doves, each of which displayed a brood patch – a patch of featherless skin on the upper breast, well supplied with blood vessels to ensure a better transmission of bodily warmth during the nesting season. The weather remained unstable. Sometimes flurries of snow would gust over the sea, then minutes later the sky would clear once more.

At midday, the first iceberg appeared, glinting majestically in the sun. The colossus was surrounded by a fine blue haze, while crevasses and caves in the surface showed a deep cobalt blue. Spray foamed over the peaks of ice. Though this spume had appeared dazzlingly white atop the waves, it looked grey and yellowish when set against the iceberg. In the afternoon, clouds began to gather; otherwise, there was nothing to be seen. Krech cursed the mariners of old 'in robust nautical fashion,' Chun noted, agreeing with the captain that the search would only continue until sunset.

Suddenly, there came a shout from the first officer: 'The Bouvets are directly ahead of us!' It was half past three and all hands rushed up on deck, dashing to the bows, to the railings and high up on the bridge. In front of them lay 'with blurred contours that soon grew clearer, just seven nautical miles ahead of us to starboard, a precipitous island in all its Antarctic majesty and wildness. To the north, the land dropped away with sheer, vertiginous cliffs and mighty glaciers that plummeted right down to sea level, while on its southern side a huge snowfield sloped gently down and ended in a sheer wall of ice that dropped into the sea; the high ridges of the island were shrouded in cloud.' In the ocean, they spotted sea anemones and sea pens, and netted mussels, chitons and crabs.

The *Valdivia* spent the next day circumnavigating the island. The researchers measured it as 5.1 nautical miles in length and 4.3 wide; the revised coordinates were 54° 26' South and 3° 24' East. There were no signs of any trees or rivers. The sea was far too rough to attempt a landing – and besides, the coastline was made up of a series of steep, forbidding cliffs of ice. The island's most prominent feature was a volcanic cone. Chun christened it Kaiser Wilhelm Peak – after all, the German emperor had shown great interest in the expedition. Chun mused that the distance south from the equator to Bouvet Island must be the same as the distance north from it to the German island of Rügen in the Baltic; you just had to imagine a Rügen covered in snow all year round, with glaciers running down to the sea and with dense pack ice surrounding the island even at the height of summer.

On Sunday 27 November, which was meant to be the crew's rest day, the ship set off in search of the other islands. Overnight, they headed north through heavy driving snow, and by six o'clock in the morning, they found themselves at the place where Thompson Island should have been situated, though they could see nothing and measured the ocean depth as 1,849 metres. However, the sea floor struck them as being flat enough for a volcanic island to have risen steeply up from the ocean at that point. They cruised about within a radius of 10 nautical miles from the given position. All the while, the sea raged, snowflakes flew by horizontally and the rigging was coated with a thick layer of ice.

And so they returned to Bouvet Island. 'We were prevented from casting one last glance at her by a dense veil of cloud that covered it, jealously shielding it from our gaze. It was then that we understood how Ross could find no trace of it, although it is clear from the course that he logged so precisely that he must have passed within four nautical miles of it!' wrote Chun. The British explorer James Ross had searched in vain for the islands in hazy and foggy conditions in 1843. Chun was therefore loath to exclude the possibility that other islands might still be out there in this vast expanse of ocean.

Later, it would transpire that Jean-Baptiste Charles Bouvet de Lozier and James Lindsay must have sighted one and the same island. In honour of its first discoverer, its name remains Bouvet. On the other hand, Liverpool Island, Bouvet-Hay and Thompson Island never existed: at the locations where they are supposed to be, the ocean is more than 2,400 metres deep.

TRIVIA

In 1927, the Norwegian Harald Horntvedt, captain of the research ship *Norvegia*, occupied the uninhabited Bouvet Island. Following a series of diplomatic negotiations, the island was declared a dependency of Norway in 1930. It is covered almost entirely by a glacier and its highest mountain is the 780-metre-high Olavtoppen.

BREASIL · ATLANTIC OCEAN

[O'BRAZILE, HY BRASIL, HY BEREASIL, BRAZIL ROCK, BRACILE]

Position west of Ireland

Size uncertain

Sightings John Nisbet (1674)

Maps Angelino Dulcert (1325),

Andrea Bianco (1436), John Purdy (1825)

BREASIL

IRELAND

The fog lifted on just a single day over the course of seven years. In an instant, a paradise-like island was revealed. Plants were in full bloom, sweet fruit hung down from the trees and the ground was studded with sparkling jewels. The first reports of such an island came from Celtic monks in the 6th century. It was said that it lay hidden in the Atlantic somewhere off the west coast of Ireland. Its name, which combines the Irish Gaelic words *breas* and *ail*, means 'great and wonderful' or 'magnificently splendid.' The ancient Irish had also once given the name Breasil to a divine being.

For a long time, the island remained nothing but a myth in the oral tradition. When it was finally written down, people started to believe in its existence. Eventually, in the 14th century, Breasil found its way onto a portolan map (an early maritime chart). The geographer Angelino Dulcert, who hailed from the Balearic island of Majorca, situated Bracile (as he called it) just a few dozen nautical miles west of Ireland. His almost-completely white map was only of use for seafarers, containing as it did nothing more than the outlines of coasts; the locations of ports, capes, dangerous rocks and sand banks; and local prevailing winds. Portolan maps evolved from Italian pilots' books, which initially noted lists of ports and instructions on how to navigate dangerous passages. It was only with the invention of the magnetic compass in the 12th century that this information could be supplemented with sketch maps of coastlines. Perhaps Dulcert was simply giving credence to a sailor's tale when he included the island on his map; since time immemorial, seafarers have been known for recounting things they either have heard from others or claim to have experienced at first hand.

Thereafter, Breasil began to appear on various maps. It was sometimes depicted in the form of a ring, like a reef, with smaller islands at its centre, and sometimes as a pair of larger twin islands. And its name changed as frequently as its shape: Brasil, Hy Bereasil, Hy Breasail, Hy Breasal. It continued to be shown on maps for more than 500 years – longer than any other phantom island. However, on maps, the island steadily migrated father and farther out into the Atlantic, as though it were trying to flee from being discovered. As early as 1436, on a map created by the Venetian Andrea Bianco, it already appeared far further to the south and was marked as 'Insula de Brasil,' alongside a larger island that formed part of the Azores.

In the late 15th century, a number of expeditions embarked from England to try to locate the island. Yet it was not until 1674 that it was finally found by Captain John Nisbet of Killybegs. What's more, he found it in the place where it was originally thought to be. Nisbet had spent several days sailing through a fog bank off the coast of Ireland when suddenly the fog lifted. 'Rocks ahead!' Nisbet cried in alarm, and ordered his ship to heave to and drop anchor. Taking three of his men, he rowed across to the island. They saw sheep, black hares and a castle. They knocked on the door of the building, but no one opened or responded. In the evening, they lit a fire on the beach – and all of a sudden, a terrible clamour arose. Nisbet and his men promptly took flight and rowed back to the ship. The following day, they ventured onto the island once more. On the beach were a number of old men, dressed in old-fashioned clothes and using the language of a bygone age. They explained that they had been kept prisoner in the castle and that Nisbet's campfire the previous evening had finally broken the spell that held them captive. The castle, they continued, had now collapsed into ruins. They said that the island was called O'Brazile. Nisbet took the men on board his ship and ferried them to his estate at Killybegs.

Breasil was never seen again; perhaps it still lies hidden in a fog bank. Thenceforth, the island shrank in size on maps. In its final appearance in the British hydrographer John Purdy's *Memoir, descriptive and explanatory, of the Northern Atlantic Ocean* (1825), it is simply called 'Brazil Rock' and is nothing more than a solitary outcrop in the sea.

ICELAND

BUSS · ATLANTIC OCEAN
[BUS, BUSSE ISLAND]

BUSS

Position 57° 1' North, in some cases also 58° 39' North
Size 150 kilometres long
Sightings James Newton (1578),
James Hall (1606), Thomas Shepherd (1671)
Maps Emery Molyneux (1592),
John Seller (1671), Keith Johnston (1856)

IRELAND

GREAT
BRITAIN

The *Emmanuel* remained behind alone off the coast of North America. She had sprung a leak and been abandoned by the expedition led by the English Elizabethan seafarer Martin Frobisher, who had sailed in search of a northwest passage around North America. '*The Busse of Bridgewater* [another name for the *Emmanuel*] was left in Bear's Sounde […] the second day of September, behind the Fleete, in some distresse through much winde, and forced there to ride it out upon the hazard of her cables and ankers, which were all aground but two,' reported Thomas Wiars, who was travelling with Frobisher on board the *Emmanuel*. The following day, 3 September 1578, saw fair weather once more. The leak in the *Emmanuel* was patched to some degree, and the return journey to England commenced.

Less than a week later, on 8 September, the ship reached the island of Frisland (see p. 66), south of Iceland. Out on the open sea, the wind turned to the south. The next morning, the *Emmanuel* set a southeasterly course for two days in the direction of Ireland.

On the 12th day of their return voyage, the crew repeatedly reported seeing drift ice in the sea, and at around 11 o'clock in the morning, they sighted land some 25 kilometres away. James Newton, the captain and owner of the vessel, promptly named the island Buss after the ship type of which the *Emmanuel* was an example – an extremely seaworthy merchant vessel. He calculated that, at the time of the first sighting, Frisland must have been situated some 150 nautical miles northwest of Buss. The southernmost part of the island was at latitude 57° 1' North, and there were two natural harbours. Buss, he stated, measured 75 nautical miles in length, and only disappeared from view after they had been underway for 28 hours.

Buss appeared on a map for the first time 14 years later, when the English mathematician Emery Molyneux included it on his globe of 1592. Despite the fact that the *Emmanuel* had only sailed along the island's southern coast, Molyneux depicted a complete coastline, as if the whole island had been circumnavigated and mapped.

Buss was seen again in 1606 by James Hall, a chief pilot in the service of King Christian IV of Denmark: 'On 1 July we sighted land at a distance of eight leagues; off its southwestern coast there lay a great ice field.' For the entire evening and night, they sailed past land that he 'supposed to be Busse Island, lying more to the westward than it is placed in the marine charts.'

In 1671, Buss was visited for a third time when the British Royal hydrographer John Seller travelled to the island, though he found it to be a few nautical miles further north. Seller was sailing under the command of Captain Thomas Shepherd, who reported seeing whales, walruses, seals and cod in great numbers. Shepherd believed that it was only possible to make two voyages to this sea area a year. Buss itself was low-lying and flat to the south, with some hills and mountains at its northwestern end. Seller sketched a rough map of the island and identified 12 locations, almost all of which he named after directors of the Hudson's Bay Company.

On 13 May 1675, the company was granted sole rights over the island by the British monarch. Sixty-five pounds were paid to Charles II for the entire island – which lay between the latitudes of 57° and 59° North – together with all sea inlets, small islands, rivers, watercourses and straits. The agreement, which was meant to apply in perpetuity, also gave the Company the right to hunt and trade in whales, sturgeon and all other 'royal' fish. All sites for the extraction of gold, silver and precious stones were likewise the property of the Hudson's Bay Company.

On that very same day, Shepherd projected the costs of investigating and exploiting the island's resources, working out the numbers of ships and men and the quantity of materials that would be required, along with all the salaries and other outgoings.

Months later, Shepherd set sail for Buss. He crossed the Atlantic and overwintered in Hudson Bay. Thereafter, there appears to have been a sudden decline of interest in Buss. Presumably the lure of the New World was so great that it simply slipped from people's minds.

Nowhere are there any reports of a systematic search for the island. Indeed, Buss is mentioned only once more by an employee of the Hudson's Bay Company, in a communiqué that prompted no further action.

By the time seven decades had passed, no one believed that the island had ever existed. A Dutch map of 1745 included a dismissive legend: *'t versonken land van BUS is hedendaags als Branding ¼ Myl lang met hol water. Is wel eer het groote Eyland Freesland geweest* ('The sunken island of Buss is nowadays nothing more than a sand bar a quarter of a mile long in the rough sea. In all probability this was once the famous island of Frisland'). The label 'sunken island of Buss' was taken up by subsequent mapmakers.

In the 18th century, British naval vessels were engaged in studying ocean and sea floor conditions west of Ireland. On the afternoon of 29 June 1776, the sea was calm in the area where Buss was once thought to have been located. Lieutenant Richard Pickersgill duly took soundings and initially touched ground at 320 fathoms. His log then stated: 'Drifted to the NE about two miles and sounded again in 290 fathoms, fine white sand; at the same time saw a shag, gulls and other signs of land not far from hence.' Pickersgill speculated that, if Buss were to reappear, 'ships heading north might overwinter there; the island would prove itself a fine training ground for hardy sailors.'

Buss Island appeared on a map for one last time in 1856, as a tiny nameless pinprick at roughly the same location as the original 'sighting.'

BYERS AND
MORRELL ISLANDS
PACIFIC OCEAN

Position 28° 32' North, 177° 4' East (Byers);
29° 57' North, 174° 31' East (Morrell)
Size both islands around 6.5 kilometres in circumference
Sightings Benjamin Morrell (1825)
Maps *Times Atlas of the World* (1922)

The American sea captain Benjamin Morrell was an ardent devotee of adventure stories and travel writing. His cabin was piled high with the works of James Cook, George Vancouver and other great navigators. In 1825, Morrell was exploring the Pacific on board his schooner *Tartar*. He sailed from east to west, passed the Hawaiian Islands and continued farther to the northeast, crossing the 180th meridian (the International Date Line) on 12 July. The International Date Line is an arbitrary line running through the Pacific from the North Pole to the South Pole. Every ship that crosses it while travelling from east to west – say, from America to China – finds itself in the following day, whereas vessels heading in the opposite direction – from west to east – sail into the previous day.

On 13 July, Morrell sighted an unknown island. Now he would finally go down in the annals of his country as a discoverer! The island was located at 28° 32' North, 177° 4' East and was extremely low-lying. The Captain could make out some scrubby vegetation and small plants, seabirds, sea turtles and elephant seals. He estimated the circumference of the island as being four miles. He also spotted a good place, which had a sandy bottom, to drop anchor. The only dangerous point was in the southeast, where a coral reef stretched for two miles southwest into the sea. Aside from this, there was not much to see. Morrell named the island after his sponsor, the New York shipowner James Byers.

Morrell did not remain on Byers Island for long. On the same day, he weighed anchor and sailed on, taking a northwesterly course. At around 4 o'clock on the morning of the following day, his crew spotted breakers ahead. They tacked for an hour to the southwest before coming about and making for a reef. By 6 o'clock, they had proceeded half a mile into the surf, but there was still no land in sight. They sailed around the western end of a coral reef, moving ahead gingerly at just seven nautical miles an hour. Finally, a lookout on the mainmast saw land to the northwest. Around 10 o'clock, they approached a narrow, flat island. There were seabirds everywhere and elephant seals lined the shore. 'We also saw an abundance of sea turtles and two hawksbill turtles,' Morrell wrote. The island was of volcanic origin, he ascertained, but scarcely rose above sea level. Its circumference was also about four miles and the centre of the island was at 29° 57' North, 174° 31' East. As he had not found anything of value, Morrell resolved to abandon the island – which would shortly come to bear his name – 'to its solitude.'

When Benjamin Morrell returned to New York, he was fired by his employer. James Byers had hoped Morrell's voyages would yield discoveries of commercial value; what was he supposed to do with a useless island named after him?

Yet the Byers and Morrell Islands did make it onto maps. As late as 1875, five full decades after their discovery, the islands survived an official 'stocktaking' of the Pacific Ocean. Sir Frederick Evans, the newly appointed hydrographer to the Royal Navy, conducted a review of Admiralty Chart 2683 – which showed the entire Pacific – and, after comparing countless ships' logbooks, expunged no fewer than 123 dubious islands. In the process, however, he made five errors: he removed from the map three islands that really did exist and retained Byers and Morrell, in spite of the fact that many mariners had raised doubts over their existence.

Perhaps Evans was concerned not to provoke a diplomatic incident. Although Byers and Morrell supposedly lay west of the 180th meridian, the United States had insisted that the International Date Line in the Northern Pacific should bulge out westward so as to ensure that the day ended on its two putative islands. They only disappeared from maritime charts in 1907, and in 1910, the International Date Line in the Northern Pacific was straightened somewhat – though to this day it is still not completely straight. Other institutions were slower to catch up: the islands could still be seen on the Pacific map in the second edition of the authoritative *Times Atlas of the World* in 1922.

By that time, Morrell (who died in 1839) was widely regarded as a consummate fantasist. It had long been known that he had not just eagerly devoured the works of earlier explorers like James Cook and George Vancouver but had even lifted sections from their logbooks verbatim. He was driven partly by a desire to embellish his own reports and partly by the dream of making major discoveries of his own. By the end of his life, Morrell was already derided as the Great Fabulist of the Pacific – a kind of American Baron Münchhausen. Yet his contemporary critics remained oblivious to the fact that Morrell had put another story out into the world that they had thus far failed to see through: for a long time, there remained on maps an island of his invention in the Weddell Sea known as New South Greenland (see p. 98).

CALIFORNIA

Isla de Parraros

Isla San Marco

CALIFORNIA
PACIFIC OCEAN

[BAJA CALIFORNIA, LOWER CALIFORNIA]

Position off the west coast of Mexico
Size uncertain
Sightings 1533
Maps John Speed (1626)

During the night of 28 November 1533, the conspirators assembled on deck. They took one final look around and nodded to one another, then Fortún Ximénez – the helmsman of the ship *Concepción* – along with his brother and a group of fellow Basques ran towards the cabin of the ship's captain, an evil-tempered brute by the name of Diego de Becerra. With daggers drawn, they kicked in the doors. Becerra woke up and leapt out of bed, but they set upon him, raining down blows on his head, arms and upper thighs. The Captain cried out, stumbled backwards and toppled onto his bunk, where the mutineers bound his bloodied body with chains. They then proceeded to storm the cabins of the other Spanish officers, thrusting with their weapons and striking almost all of the men dead.

Ximénez now had full command of the galleon. For the past month, the ship had been sailing north along the Pacific coast of Mexico in search of a legendary land of gold, which had been described two decades earlier by the writer Garci Rodríguez de Montalvo, and a strait that was rumoured to lead from the Pacific into the Atlantic Ocean. Spanish geographers asserted the existence of such a passage, the so-called Strait of Anián. It was presumed to lie not so very far from the equator. If found, it would render the long and arduous voyage around the tip of South America redundant. It would also make the sea route from Spain to China much shorter.

In December, Ximénez found himself sailing into a wide gulf. To starboard, he could see the continental mainland and likewise a stretch of land to port, which he christened Baja California. He was convinced that it was an island.

'Know that on the right hand from the Indies there lies an island called California, very close to the region of the Earthly Paradise,' fantasised Montalvo in his novel of 1510, *Las Sergas de Esplandián* ('The Exploits of Esplandián'). He recounted that the island was peopled by Black women, with not a single man among them, who lived in the manner of Amazons. They were robust of stature, possessed great strength and spirited courage and were extremely virtuous. Montalvo continued: 'Their weapons are all made of gold, as is the armour of the wild beasts that they captured, tamed, and rode. The whole island is full of gold and precious stones, because there is no metal except gold here.' The ruler of the island was called Califia, a queen of majestic proportions, more beautiful than all the others and in the full bloom of her womanhood. She longed to win renown through great deeds, and she was known to be spirited, daring and passionately valiant. Five hundred griffins – half-eagle and half-lion – protected this race of women. These fearsome beasts swooped down on any man who dared approach, and devoured him.

Convinced that he had found Montalvo's island, Ximénez took the chance of rowing over to Baja California with a party of 21 men to find fresh water. The rest of the crew watched helplessly from the deck of the galleon as local natives armed with spears suddenly appeared and slaughtered Ximénez and his companions.

The *Concepción* hastily set sail, turned to the south and some weeks later arrived at the Pacific port of Acapulco. There, the survivors told their commander, the Spanish conquistador Hernán Cortés, about the great misfortune that had befallen the others on the shoreline of Baja California.

Just six years later, in 1539, Francisco de Ulloa was despatched to once more attempt to find the legendary Strait of Anián in the name of Cortés. Ulloa left the harbour at Acapulco on 8 July with a fleet of three ships. The entire way, he hugged the coastline, venturing far up into the wide inlet that separates Baja California from Mexico. But, as he proceeded, this body of water grew steadily narrower all the way up to the mouth of the Colorado River in the far north, where it transpired that the supposed strait was in fact a dead end. It was therefore not the Strait of Anián, but simply a vast bay of incalculable size.

Ulloa turned around and sailed south, keeping hard up against the shore of Baja California as he went; rounding its southern tip, he then proceeded to sail north along the Pacific coast. One of his ships, the

Santo Tomás, was sunk in a storm. He continued his expedition with the remaining two vessels but, during another violent storm, the *Trinidad* vanished without trace.

Back in Acapulco, the crew of the third ship, the *Santa Agueda*, reported the loss of the other vessels and told of their disappointment on discovering that Baja California was nothing but an elongated peninsula. Henceforth, it appeared in its correct form on the maps produced by all the leading European geographers. And that should have been the end of the story...

However, in the late 16th century, new life was breathed into the myth: sailing under the Spanish flag, the Greek sailor Juan de Fuca (whose real name was Ioannis Phokas) explored the western seaboard of North America. Back home in Europe, he boasted of having found the Strait of Anián. The strait was situated between 47° and 48° North, he claimed, and it took barely 20 days to sail through it to the Atlantic Ocean; this proved that Baja California was an island after all. Furthermore, de Fuca maintained that the area around the strait was 'very fertile, and rich in gold, silver and pearls.' Soon after, news of his account reached London and duly did the rounds of the cartographers there.

In 1626, the British mapmaker John Speed published a brilliant map of the New World. Never before had its coasts been shown so accurately. In addition, around the margin of the map, Speed included eight detailed cityscapes and 10 vignettes of Native Americans. On the back, however, he wrote disparagingly about their 'barbarian' customs and their propensity for idolatry. Otherwise, he asked, how could they possibly have taken ordinary Europeans for gods? The indigenous peoples of the Americas were savages, he claimed, and 'their tendency to violence appears to have sprung from Hell itself.' Speed's map shaped the popular image of the New World, yet it contained another flaw: on it, Baja California was still shown as an island.

The myth persisted in people's minds for a further eight decades. Then, in the closing years of the 17th century, the Jesuit missionary Eusebio Francisco Kino conclusively proved that Baja California was just a peninsula. Among his other accomplishments, Kino had spent some time in southern Germany studying theology, mathematics and astronomy. In the spring of 1681, he arrived in Pimería Alta, a region to the north of the Spanish colonies in the Americas, and immediately began establishing mission stations. For more than two decades, Kino explored the region, created a network of paths and walked as far as the Colorado River, which flowed into the great bay between the mainland and the peninsula. In 1702, Kino drew a map on which he included this discovery and sent a copy to Paris, where it was published in a Jesuit periodical and was later reproduced in Denis Diderot's famous *Encyclopédie*.

All the same, the legend persisted in America. As late as 1746, an expedition set off from Mexico with the express intention of proving to the world that Baja California was an island – but failed when it came up against the reality of the situation. Thus, it took until the mid-18th century to finally prove beyond all doubt that no fabulous island of Amazons existed in the far west of North America.

CROCKER LAND
ARCTIC OCEAN

Position 83° North, 100° West

Size uncertain

Sightings Peary (1906), MacMillan (1914)

Maps undated (c.1910)

In mid-April 1914, misty conditions with overcast skies prevailed north of Greenland. In the company of two explorer-companions and a pair of Inuit guides, Donald Baxter MacMillan was approaching the point from which Crocker Land had first been sighted. This was a mysterious location, which MacMillan had called the last great geographical enigma of the North. On 21 April, the skies finally cleared.

And indeed: there was some land! All of a sudden, MacMillan was able to make out an outline beginning in the southwest and stretching far to the northeast, occupying virtually the whole horizon. He reached for his binoculars, focussed them and saw white valleys and snow-capped peaks. He was enthralled, and his two companions cheered; now they could finally be certain that their expedition would be a success. Only their Inuit guides remained silent and sceptical.

MacMillan's expedition was supported by the American Museum of Natural History, the American Geographical Society and the University of Illinois. To accompany him on his journey, he had selected a team of highly skilled young researchers, including a geologist, a zoologist and a geophysicist, as well as a radio operator and a mechanic, who was also responsible for cooking. In addition, he had with him a young Inuk man who had been brought to New York by a previous expedition and who would serve as MacMillan's interpreter.

The team set off from New York on 2 July 1913. By mid-August, they had reached Etah in the far northwest of Greenland, the most northerly settlement in the world that had not been established solely as a scientific research station. With the help of some Inuit hired hands, they erected a building there with eight rooms and storage space. Henceforth, the only messages that the researchers would receive would come to them by dog sled.

On 10 March 1914, MacMillan – along with Fitzhugh Green Sr. and Walter Elmer Ekblaw – set off to the north, where Crocker Land was supposed to lie. This gigantic island had only been discovered a few years before, in 1906. According to the polar explorer Robert Peary, it was situated at 83° North, 100° West in the Canadian Arctic Archipelago, some 210 kilometres north of the Canadian territory of Ellesmere Island and northwest of Greenland. From there, it was not far to the North Pole. Peary named the island after his financial backer, the American businessman George Crocker, who had made his fortune in real estate, railways and banking.

MacMillan's group was accompanied by seven Inuit porters carrying two tonnes of equipment on dog sleds. The temperature was -45°C and a journey of 2,000 kilometres lay ahead of them. In order to economise on provisions, the porters were sent back one by one to the base station at Etah.

Five weeks after their departure, on the morning of 14 April, Green, MacMillan and the Inuit guides Peea-wah-to and E-tooka-shoo – Ekblaw having left the party by now – ventured out onto the frozen sea of ice. Their dog sleds made swift progress across it. After a week, on the morning of 21 April, Green rushed to the door of the igloo they had constructed and cried out: 'We have it!' On the horizon, the faint contours of hills, valleys and mountain peaks could be identified: Crocker Land!

For five days thereafter, MacMillan's team pressed farther north, eventually reaching the point that Peary had only seen from a distance. At the time, he had thought it was a 1,000-metre peak. MacMillan looked around, but saw nothing. Frustrated, he set off on the return route with the others, turning around frequently as he proceeded and noting in his diary that evening: 'Throughout the day the mirage generated by the ice sea made it look like an immense area of land; it seemed to mock us. It appeared so close and so easy to reach, if only we'd just turn around and go back.' In resignation, he added: 'My dreams of the past four years were merely dreams, my hopes had ended in bitter disappointment.'

Scarcely had they reached dry land when the ice started to crack behind them. Deep fissures opened up, and ice floes began to drift apart. What a stroke of fortune that they had turned around in good time! They had not gone far, though, before icebergs reared up in front of them. While MacMillan and E-tooka-shoo headed straight back in the direction of Etah, Green and Peea-wah-to sped off on their dog sleds to explore another unknown region. Only one of them would return from this excursion.

As they travelled, a blizzard suddenly blew up, whipping snow directly into their faces. Peea-wah-to quickly constructed an igloo. But time and again, the narrow entrance became blocked with driving snow, causing them to almost suffocate inside. After the storm had abated, Green went in search of his dogs. He found them buried under three metres of snow, frozen stiff. But at least his Inuk guide's dogs had managed to survive. Panting from the effort, Green harnessed himself to his sled and dragged it along behind Peea-wah-to, who presently started to pull farther and farther ahead. Green was groaning and sweating. Eventually he pulled out a .22 calibre rifle from his sled and ordered the Inuk guide to stay behind him. But when, soon after this incident, Green glanced round, he saw Peea-wah-to making off in a different direction. In his journal, the American noted: 'I shot once in the air. He did not stop. I then killed him with a shot through the shoulder and another through the head.' Green eventually returned to base on his own.

MacMillan's men were trapped on the icy waste for several months. In order to requisition a rescue ship, in December 1914, MacMillan set off on a dog sled for southern Greenland accompanied by Maurice Cole Tanquary. From there, he would be able to make radio contact with the United States, but ahead of them lay a journey of 650 kilometres. On the way, they got lost and wandered about uselessly for 10 days, seriously depleting their food supplies. When one of their dogs died, they skinned it and scraped the meat off its bones. Finally, they reached an Inuit settlement, where Tanquary very carefully began to remove his boots; they had virtually welded onto his skin. His feet were covered in blood and stank from the effects of frostbite, with scraps of decomposing muscle tissue hanging loose. He promptly tugged his boots back on and headed straight back to Etah, where he had his big toes surgically removed.

In the summer of 1915, the American Museum of Natural History despatched a rescue ship to the Arctic. However, the schooner became trapped in pack ice, as did a second vessel they sent the following year. It was 1917 before MacMillan and his men were finally rescued. On 24 August 1917, they landed in Nova Scotia off the Atlantic coast of Canada. Their expedition had been a scientific disappointment and a financial disaster. The initial estimate of the expedition's cost was 52,000 American dollars; in the event, it had cost almost twice that sum. MacMillan returned with only very few scientific findings. All he could say about Crocker Land was that it had dissolved into thin air.

Perhaps MacMillan should have guessed that phantom islands were wont to pop up in northern climes. A similar phenomenon had occurred once before, almost a century previously, in 1818, when the Scottish rear admiral John Ross sailed into Arctic waters in search of the fabled Northwest Passage – a navigable sea route to the East around the north of the North American continent. Ross was some 350 nautical miles south of Etah when he abandoned his quest and turned about. In the distance, he thought he had seen a mountainous tract of land barring his onward route. He named it after the First Secretary to the Admiralty, John Wilson Croker. It was sheer historical coincidence that the illusory island in search of which MacMillan embarked had such a similar name, albeit relating to a totally different person.

DEVIL'S ISLAND
ATLANTIC OCEAN

[SATANAZES, SATANZES, ISLA DE LOS DEMONIOS]

Position variously west of the Azores, close to Greenland,
or off South America
Size initially as large as Switzerland, then progressively smaller
Sightings uncertain
Maps Zuane Pizzigano (1424), Johannes Ruysch (1508)

Juan

DEVIL'S ISLAND

FRISLAND

IRELAND

GREAT
BRITAIN

Breasil

IBERIA

Azores

Even sources as old as the Norse myths make mention of a 'Devil's Island.' Some tales speak of a gigantic hand suddenly rearing up from the ocean and snatching ships, while others talk of the gruesome noises made by huge monsters living on barren, rocky coasts. Even Christopher Columbus cited accounts of extraordinary creatures, such as men with muzzles like dogs, who ate humans, and others whose foreheads each bore a single, huge eye. He had not seen these at first hand, however. Another explorer, the English navigator Henry Hudson, claimed to have himself come across a mermaid in the Arctic in 1608: her back and breasts were like those of a woman, and she had a body the same size as a person's, though her skin was chalky white.

To begin with, the Devil's Island was located close to the coast of mainland Europe. The cartographer Zuane Pizzigano drew a rectangular island in the Atlantic just west of Spain on his portolan chart of 1424, noting above it in block letters: *ista ixola dimexo satanazes* – 'this island is called Devil's Island.' He used the evil Satan as the logical counterpart to the devout Catholic island of Antilia (see p. 12) nearby.

And just as the Devil is famously able to do, the island of Satanazes constantly changed shape throughout the 16th century. The astronomer and geographer Johannes Ruysch depicted an almond-shaped double island called Isla de los Demonios on his map of 1508. He may even have ventured there in person: the double island lay off Newfoundland, at that time still a little-explored region. Next to it – as though he had witnessed such a thing with his own eyes – Ruysch wrote on his map: 'Devils attack ships that sail too close to the island.' Could he have just been referring to screaming seagulls?

French sailors also reported sighting a satanic island close to Newfoundland. The first thing they heard, the story goes, was an inarticulate hubbub of human voices; they felt sure that demons were vying with one another over who should be first to torment the mortals. These fiends reputedly attacked every ship that came near, and pursued anyone crazy enough to set foot on the island.

In the mid-16th century, a remarkable story ended up doing the rounds of the fashionable literary salons of Paris. A noblewoman by the name of Marguerite de la Rocque de Roberval recounted how she had travelled to America as a young girl on board a ship captained by her uncle, Sieur de Roberval. He had been tasked with establishing the first French colony in the New World in the name of the king. On the voyage, Marguerite had fallen in love with a common sailor and, as a result, she, her lover and her maid had been put ashore on a barren island. There, she claimed, they had been plagued at night by satanic demons flying through the air. Her paramour subsequently died, along with the maid. She alone had been rescued by a ship and brought back to France.

While Devil's Island gradually disappeared from maps with the passage of time, the French botanist Jean-Baptiste Thibault de Chanvalon embarked on an expedition to South America in 1763. Off the northeast coast of the continent, he discovered a tiny unknown island that he christened Île du Diable ('Island of the Devil'). He could not have imagined that it would later gain notoriety as a penal colony. For Alfred Dreyfus, its most famous prisoner, Île du Diable truly did become a hell on Earth. The French former artillery officer arrived on the island on 13 April 1895. He had been convicted of high treason and publicly stripped of his military rank. Dreyfus was forced to spend four years living in a hut measuring only four square metres. He was forbidden to speak to the guards, lost weight drastically and suffered repeated bouts of malarial fever. And when the French government improbably began to fear that he might escape, he was shackled to his bed and a tall palisade was erected around his hut. The fact that Dreyfus was innocent of all the charges and that he had been wrongly incarcerated on Île du Diable was only officially acknowledged many years later.

FRISLAND
NORTH ATLANTIC OCEAN

[FRISSLAND, FRISCHLANT, FRIESLAND, FREEZELAND,
FRISLANDIA, FIXLAND]

Position southern coast between 60° and 61° North

Size similar to that of Ireland

Sightings mid-14th century

Maps Nicolò Zeno the Younger (1558), Gerardus Mercator (1569),
The English Atlas (1680)

The mid-16th century saw the publication in Venice of a slim volume containing a curious story and a nautical map. In it, Nicolò Zeno the Younger recounted the tale of an astonishing voyage undertaken by his forebears. According to the story, two centuries earlier, the intrepid nobleman Nicolò Zeno the Elder – who loved adventure and travel – had set sail from his home city of Venice. In 1380, he ventured out into the Atlantic Ocean through the Strait of Gibraltar and soon found himself caught in a violent storm to the west of the British Isles. After days of aimless drifting, his ship finally ran aground on the shores of an unknown island.

As the inhabitants of the island prepared to attack, a prince suddenly came into view. He commanded the attackers to disperse, and then struck up a conversation with the sailors in Latin. He was delighted to learn that they came from Italy, and bade his guests welcome on Frisland. The prince, who held sway over a number of islands, introduced himself to them as Zichmni and took Zeno into service on board his own ship. Before long, Zeno had captured a number of small islands, commandeered several vessels and explored uncharted waters in the region, as well as being granted a knighthood by Prince Zichmni. Together, they took up residence in the island's capital, from whose harbour fish were exported in huge quantities to Flanders, England, Norway and Denmark.

One day, Nicolò wrote to his brother, Antonio, urging him to leave Venice and come to join him on Frisland. Some weeks later, the two brothers were embracing one another joyfully, and soon joined forces to overrun the islands of Estland, Talas, Broas, Iscant, Trans, Mimant, Dambere and Bres. Under Zichmni's command, they even landed on Iceland, though they failed in their attempt to conquer the island after its inhabitants dug in behind high defensive walls. The brothers then sailed farther north to Greenland. The book does not specify exactly where they made land, but in the distance, they could see a mountain spewing out fire. All the houses there were built of lava stone and had gardens full of flowers, herbs and fruit. The brothers came across monks of the Dominican order and saw a church dedicated to Saint Thomas, which was heated by water from a hot spring. In the course of the nine months that winter lasted there, Nicolò Zeno fell ill, but he made it back to Frisland before dying.

Antonio inherited his brother's fortune and begged Zichmni to allow him to return to Italy. However, he was refused permission; the prince still had plans for him. Some 1,600 kilometres west of Frisland, fishermen had discovered a rich island called Estotiland. On their return, they told tales of castles, a writing system and gold mines, as well as grain plantations, beer and sailing ships. The only thing the people there lacked, apparently, was the mariner's compass.

To help Zichmni locate this island, Antonio was ordered to come with him as captain on a great voyage. According to the story, they journeyed to Ledovo, explored the Icarian Sea and sailed on westward to an idyllic island. There, they dropped anchor in a wide bay, wandered across green meadows and saw a smoking mountain. They stared in amazement at the huge shoals of fish, the fertile soil and the cave-dwelling inhabitants, who were wild, timid and small in stature. Zichmni remained on the island and founded a city there. Antonio, however, was ordered to take all the crew members who did not wish to stay there back to Frisland.

For 20 days, Antonio headed in the direction of Frisland from Estotiland, before changing course and sailing southeast for five days. He landed on the island of Neome, from where it was just a short step to Frisland. This is where the story ended.

In the afterword to the book, Nicolò Zeno the Younger wrote that he had chanced upon his ancestor's letters as a child. After reading them, he had torn the originals into pieces. He admitted ruefully that he had, after all, only been a small boy at the time: 'I recall this incident now with feelings of great shame.' Yet he was determined that the story of his forebears should not be lost to posterity. Along with his 1558 book, he also reproduced a detailed map of the North Atlantic. On it, Frisland appears larger than Ireland. He kept the original map at home, together with some other artefacts, he explained, and claimed that it was simple to decipher.

The cartographers of Europe were astonished at Zeno's map; many details looked extremely plausible. In 1569, the renowned mapmaker Gerardus Mercator included Frisland on his updated map of Europe, placing it south of Iceland. And Abraham Ortelius even went so far as to suggest that it was not Christopher Columbus who had discovered the New World – at least not the northern part, which was called Estotiland and which jutted out closest to Europe – or the islands of Greenland, Iceland and Frisland. The first people to set foot there, he maintained, had been fisherman from Frisland, and these places had subsequently been rediscovered by Antonio Zeno.

The English monarchy summarily claimed Frisland as a sovereign territory. 'I spake with Mr Secretary Walsingham. I declared to the Quene her title to Greenland, Estetiland and Friseland,' ran the entry for 28 November 1577 in the diary of Queen Elizabeth I's close confidant, the mathematician Dr John Dee. Dee further declared that the countries in question had in any case long since belonged to the English crown: 'Circa anno 530, Kyng Arthur did not only conquer Iseland, Greenland and all northern islands as far as the territory of the Duke of Moscovia in Russia, but his domain extended as far as the North Pole. He despatched colonists thence and to all islands between Scotland and Iseland, wherefore it is probable that the aforementioned land of Friseland constitutes an ancient English discovery and possession.'

In the 19th century, historians set about researching the story of the Zeno brothers. Every detail was dissected and examined in more than 400 articles and books. Nicolò and Antonio were indeed Venetian seafarers, however Nicolò did not die in 1394 on Frisland; in fact, that same year saw him appear as a defendant in a court case in Venice. He was accused of having embezzled money while serving as the military governor of Greece. Researchers also discovered that many details on his map had been copied from older maps that had since gone missing.

Nonetheless, the story may still have some truth to it; it could just be that the dates are wrong. Indeed, the landscapes that were described in the book are reminiscent of the Faroe Islands. And the brothers may really have seen the Icelandic volcanoes that are described in the book on their voyages. During their lifetime, there was already a cathedral in the settlement of Garðar, at that time an episcopal see situated on the fertile southern plain of Greenland. Furthermore, the author and sailor Donald Johnson has speculated that Estotiland may well have been the Labrador Peninsula, which juts out from the coastline of North America. If Irish monks did indeed ever find their way there, as has been suggested, that would explain how the people there could have communicated with fishermen from Europe in Latin.

On the other hand, the whole affair might be much more straight-forward: Nicolò Zeno the Younger lived in Venice, a place where seafarers from all around the world would call in and regale one another with adventure stories in the cheap inns along the waterfront. All Zeno needed to do was listen and note down everything he heard. Seen in this light, although his book may not have contained the true story of his forebears, it at least captured the oral storytelling tradition of his time, which would otherwise have been lost forever.

TRIVIA

In 1998, the descendants of Henry I Sinclair, Earl of Orkney (c.1345–c.1400) celebrated the 600th anniversary of the discovery of America. The family is convinced that their forebear is none other than Prince Zichmni. They claim to have found conclusive proof in Rosslyn Chapel, where the Earl is buried. This Gothic church, dating from the 15th century, is situated in the village of Roslin in Midlothian, Scotland. The roof vaulting of the building – which was constructed in 1446, crucially before the date that Christopher Columbus is generally considered to have 'discovered' America – allegedly includes carvings depicting corn (maize) cobs. At the time when the chapel was built, however, corn was still unknown in Europe and was only cultivated in the Americas. Accordingly, so the reasoning goes, Sinclair must have brought cobs of corn back to Scotland from a voyage to South America.

HARMSWORTH ISLAND
ARCTIC OCEAN

[ALFRED HARMSWORTH ISLAND]

Position 57° North

Size uncertain

Sightings 1897

Maps unclear

Albert Edward Island

HARMSWORTH ISLAND

Arthur
Island

Prince George Land

A l e x a n d r a   L a n d

Hundreds of people stood waving their handkerchiefs as the largest airship in the world emerged from its hangar at Friedrichshafen on the shores of Lake Constance at 8.35 on the morning of 24 July 1931: the LZ 127 *Graf Zeppelin* – 236.6 metres long, 30.5 metres in diameter and powered by five Otto diesel engines, each generating 2,850 horsepower. Its cruising speed was 115 kilometres per hour, and in the gondola slung beneath the airship's envelope, there were cabins for 25 passengers plus a saloon measuring five metres by six and a galley. The *Graf Zeppelin* had already flown from Germany to North America, the Far East, South America, Russia and Great Britain, and, on one occasion, it had even circumnavigated the globe.

This day, however, marked the very first journey made by a zeppelin to the Arctic; the flight would chalk up another record and also act as a brilliant marketing boost for airship travel. Under the leadership of Dr Hugo Eckener, the director of the Zeppelin Works, this expedition would chart a course via Berlin and Leningrad to the archipelago of Franz Josef Land and then on past Harmsworth Island, which was situated not far from the North Pole in the Barents Sea. The *Graf Zeppelin* would then turn east and head for the myriad islands off Siberia before finally making its return journey to Germany: a round trip of 13,000 kilometres in six days, most spent flying in sub-zero temperatures.

Eckener climbed aboard the gondola, followed by his 30-strong crew; 12 scientists from Germany, the USSR, Sweden and the United States; and three reporters, including a young man by the name of Arthur Koestler. Eckener was not just an industrialist, but the president of Aeroarctic, a society for the promotion of scientific study of the Arctic. He had been planning this expedition for many years and had met several times with Roald Amundsen, the veteran Norwegian polar explorer and the first man to reach the South Pole. Indeed, Amundsen had been meant to accompany Eckener on the flight, but he had been missing since 1928, his seaplane having disappeared without trace somewhere in the Barents Sea while searching for survivors of the airship *Italia*, which had crashed on an expedition to the North Pole.

The *Graf Zeppelin* lifted off, and the spectators waved their handkerchiefs once more in farewell. Eckener had once been a journalist himself and knew that big stories needed to be stage-managed. The original intention, therefore, had been to have the airship rendezvous with the American submarine *Nautilus* at the North Pole. The reporters on board would have had a magnificent tableau laid on for them, which they could have written about in glowing terms: airship meets submarine! At the North Pole, no less! A truly historic event! But the *Nautilus* had encountered many technical problems on her voyage from the United States to the Arctic and was eventually scuttled in a fjord in Norway. Instead, it was now planned for the airship to rendezvous with the Soviet icebreaker *Malygin* off Franz Josef Land.

No airship had ever ventured so far north before. 'The old explorers who "did it on foot" must have given thought to the airway as they gazed from the encumbered ground to the freedom of the sky,' wrote the American researchers Lincoln Ellsworth and Edward Smith, two of the scientists invited to join the Aeroarctic expedition. But the polar researchers were looking for more than just the thrill of flying over the Arctic; not least, they wanted to find out if the existing maps of the region were accurate. And they hoped in the process to find unknown islands. In the mid-20th century, where else but in the Earth's polar regions could one make such spectacular discoveries?

The travellers landed in Berlin at six o'clock in the evening. The following morning, the *Graf Zeppelin* flew on, initially heading for Helsinki before turning east toward Leningrad, where they spent another night in a hotel. As they left Leningrad, those on board the airship had a view of the city's Peter and Paul Fortress followed by a vista of lakes, forests and isolated settlements. Bit by bit, they approached the no-man's land of the Far North. By the afternoon, they were floating over Arkhangelsk, the largest timber-exporting port in the world, where floating logs choked the waterways. At around seven o'clock, they crossed the Arctic Circle. The wind blew from an easterly direction and freshened as they reached the sea. The temperature dropped as they left the more temperate climatic zone and advanced into the chill atmosphere of the Arctic. For several hours, the *Graf Zeppelin* followed the coastline, sometimes at a height of 500 metres and at other times descending to 200 metres. From their vantage point, the passengers could see timber beams lying on the shore and fish traps designed for catching salmon.

By the next morning, they had reached the Kanin Peninsula, the northernmost point on the Russian mainland. There was a fresh north-northwesterly breeze, measuring force five or six on the Beaufort scale. Ahead of them lay the Barents Sea and an ocean crossing of 2,500 kilometres to reach Franz Josef Land. To economise on fuel, Eckener ordered two of the five engines to be shut down. That night, the airship pressed onward assisted by a strong tailwind; as morning broke, the scientists could see below them the odd tree trunk floating in the sea and seabirds bobbing on the waves. The *Graf Zeppelin* drifted through patches of mist, with the outside temperature at just 4°C. The airship climbed until there was nothing but clear blue sky above it, while beneath billowed the endless folds of a white sea of fog. Later that morning, the crew radioed the *Malygin*, which was anchored off Hooker Island awaiting their arrival.

The Franz Josef Land archipelago had only been mapped for the first time four decades previously. The British polar explorer Frederick George Jackson had led an expedition to the Arctic, financed by the British newspaper and publishing magnate Alfred Harmsworth, 1st Viscount Northcliffe. Jackson spent three years, from 1894 to 1897, exploring the vast island realm of the Arctic. His pioneering journey demonstrated that the archipelago comprised a group of some 200 islands and were not one single large continent, as had previously been thought. Jackson also discovered a hitherto unknown island northwest of the archipelago, which he named after his patron, Harmsworth. Those travelling on board the *Graf Zeppelin* would be sure to see this island en route.

The *Malygin* reported over the radio that the first pack ice began north of 78° North and that otherwise gentle northeasterly winds prevailed with a light mist. Gradually, the clouds beneath the *Graf Zeppelin* began to disperse. Floating on the sea below were ice floes just one metre thick – so flat and insubstantial that they could only have formed during the winter just gone. Then the wind decreased.

In the afternoon, the southernmost islands of Franz Josef Land came into view. Cape Flora on Northbrook Island lay dead ahead, its bare rock free of glaciers. This was an unforgettable location for polar explorers; the island was easy to reach by sea, so many expeditions began their explorations from here.

At around 17.45, the *Graf Zeppelin* was circling over Hooker Island. A Soviet radio and weather station stood on a rocky outcrop, and the *Malygin* was anchored just offshore. The sea was now calm with no waves or spray, and the airship was reflected in the water, where just a few blocks of ice were drifting. Eckener ordered the inflatable pontoons to be made ready to serve as flotation rings for the giant airship. The craft began its steady descent. Thirty metres above the sea, tubs attached to ropes were let down; these filled with water, and this additional weight gently pulled the airship even lower. Finally, an anchor was dropped.

A boat was despatched from the *Malygin*. When it reached the zeppelin, brief handshakes took place between officers at the side door of the gondola and the bow of the boat. Mailbags changed hands. Some 50,000 items of mail from all over the world, weighing 300 kilograms, were handed over from the airship, which itself took on board a bag weighing 120 kilograms from the *Malygin*. (In fact, the sale of commemorative postage stamps played a large part in financing this escapade.)

Suddenly, an ice floe was spotted heading straight for the *Graf Zeppelin*; all the tubs had to be immediately emptied and the anchor lifted. Just 15 minutes after touching down, the airship ascended once more and resumed its journey, which it began with a wide detour around

Prince George Land, the largest and longest island in the archipelago. Then it set off eastwards in conditions of excellent visibility, enabling the crew to see 60 kilometres ahead.

Here, the first errors in existing maps became evident: Armitage Island was not in fact an island, but merely a peninsula of Prince George Land. The island called Albert Edward simply did not exist. Indeed, right up to the horizon, there was no land to be seen from here. 'Strange though it may sound, Harmsworth Island did not exist either. Where it should have been there was nothing but the black Arctic sea and the bright reflection of the airship gliding over it,' reported the journalist Koestler. And the researcher Ellsworth radioed the following message to the American Geographical Society at 18.45: 'Met first ice in loose fields 120 miles south of British Channel. Now circling Alexandra Island. Present chart not correct. Albert Edward Island and Harmsworth Island do not exist.' The transmission was brief and to the point. Yet the publisher Alfred Harmsworth, after whom the island was named, was spared knowing anything of all this – he had died almost a decade earlier in London.

The *Graf Zeppelin* then turned to the northeast. As a bay came into view, those on board saw a number of tiny rocky islets that had not yet been included on maps of the region. Around midnight on the fourth day of their journey, they rounded Cape Fligely on Rudolf Island – the most northerly point of their expedition and the northernmost land point of Eurasia, barely 800 kilometres from the North Pole. Eckener and Ellsworth looked to the north; there was a faint glimmer on the horizon where the midnight sun had just set. The world was bathed in a soft and gentle light, and just a solitary golden shimmering shaft of light shot briefly over the ice.

The airship slipped down to an altitude of 250 metres, passing two overlapping smoothly polished ice floes. The ice fields were studded all over with pools of meltwater, some coloured brown, green or yellow from the chlorophyll of the algae they contained or from the microscopic plankton that had been growing in them from prehistoric times. The morning of 28 July dawned with a fresh breeze. The *Graf Zeppelin* was flying through a light mist at a speed of 105 kilometres per hour. The passengers caught glimpses of the island of Severnaya Zemlya off the coast of Siberia. A rugged white landscape about which no reports existed stretched beneath the feet of the scientists. Flat glaciers merged into fields of sea ice, making it almost impossible to tell where one ended and the other began. They then flew westward over the Russian mainland, with the Taimyr Peninsula below. Here the land was tundra – brown, yellow and red. Thousands of birds were nesting around the shores of lakes, and herds of reindeer wandered across the plains, scattering in alarm when they caught sight of the airship.

Then, the airship made one more sea crossing to Novaya Zemlya, a thin 900-kilometre-long double island in the Arctic Ocean. The expedition had by now been underway for five days, and for the first time they saw Alpine glaciers. That afternoon, they flew back over the Barents Sea and in the evening passed Arkhangelsk.

The following day, they had a stopover of just half an hour at Berlin Tempelhof Airport, where thousands of onlookers came to wave them on. Then, on 31 July, the *Graf Zeppelin* slipped back virtually unnoticed into her home base at Friedrichshafen.

A number of original letters franked with the commemorative stamp of the *Graf Zeppelin*'s Arctic flight, which once helped fund the expedition, still circulate among collectors.

JUAN DE LISBOA
INDIAN OCEAN

Position 73° 36' East, 27° 34' South

Size uncertain

Sightings uncertain

Maps Johannes van Keulen (1689)

Carqados Carajos Shoals

Isla de Santa Maria

MADAGASCAR

Santa Apolonia

Do Mascarenhas

JUAN DE LISBOA

'Can't you drum up some gruesome details about people being tortured and killed?' the German imperial chancellor Otto von Bismarck enquired of his staff in the autumn of 1888. He needed a tangible reason to order the suppression of a revolt in the empire's fledgling colony of German East Africa. On the coast, ordinary people were rebelling against the brutal seizure of their land by the foreign imperialists; they preferred to remain part of the Sultanate of Zanzibar. In order to justify an intervention by the navy, Bismarck issued a public declaration that the uprising was being orchestrated by fanatical slave traders.

On 4 November of that year, Berlin sent a telegram to the German military commander in East Africa: 'The Emperor commands that a strict blockade of the mainland harbours of the Sultanate be carried out jointly with British forces in the region in order to suppress the slave trade and to prevent the influx of war material.' All suspicious vessels were to be boarded regardless of what flag they were flying and, if necessary, impounded.

By the beginning of December, the first four cruisers and gunboats of the Imperial Navy were patrolling the waters off the German colony. 'Now we're cruising up and down the coast in pursuit of dhows; every five or six weeks we sail over to Zanzibar to bunker with coal, purchase a few cans of tinned food, and then it's off once more,' noted one lieutenant. He went on to observe that the rations were frugal and that the climate was not particularly agreeable.

Over the following months, thousands of ships were stopped and searched, yet only very few of these actions yielded any results. On 5 December, for instance, the German Navy freed 87 enslaved people from a dhow, a traditional type of sailing vessel that plied these waters. In mid-December, another 146 were discovered. But these were the most spectacular successes. In both cases, cruisers towed the slave ships they had seized to the coast, where they were sawed up into pieces and displayed as a warning on the shore. The freed people were sent to various Christian missionary stations.

The most remarkable act of liberation was carried out in the Indian Ocean by the cruiser SMS *Leipzig* on Christmas Eve 1888. The German sailors boarded a dhow that was found to have five light-skinned enslaved people chained below deck. They spoke fluent French and were called Samuel, Wilhelm, Kasimir, August and Benjamin Benyovszky. Once in the care of a missionary station, they told a young padre how their great-grandfather, Maurice Benyovszky, had founded a colony on Madagascar in the late 18th century. A town of mud huts had been erected there in the name of the French King. As well as building roads, they recounted, their great-grandfather had also instigated trade with other islands and settled conflicts. The people of Madagascar had held him in such reverence that they chose him to be their king, but then the French withdrew their support for him and sent a force to attack him. In a skirmish, their great-grandfather had been wounded by a bullet to the right side of his chest. He had hidden himself in the jungle, and a few days later, according to their account, he had escaped with a number of followers on a ship to the island of Juan de Lisboa.

This island had been discovered by French sea captains in the 17th century. On a map produced in 1689 by the geographer Johannes van Keulen, it was shown east of Madagascar and was the shape of a dolphin leaping out of the water. Because the island had never been found again, it was regarded as forgotten – thus providing the perfect hideaway for the fugitives.

The great-grandchildren went on to explain to the priest that Maurice Benyovszky had been received like a god on Juan de Lisboa and was elected once more to be a ruler. He founded a city and married the daughter of a chieftain, making her his queen. Together, they established a parliament and introduced free elections. They raised several children, and for a hundred years, peace reigned on Juan de Lisboa. But then the slave traders had arrived and captured the great-grandchildren, and now they had finally been saved by the crew of the *Leipzig*. The great-grandchildren did not want to reveal the exact whereabouts of the island; when all was said and done, they stated, it would be better if it were to slip back into obscurity.

TRIVIA

It is possible that Juan de Lisboa served as the model for the fictitious island of San Serriffe, the famous April Fool's Day hoax perpetrated by the British daily newspaper *The Guardian*. On 1 April 1977, it ran a profile of the supposed island over seven pages. The catalyst for this, the journalists claimed, was the 10th anniversary of a revolution there: on 1 April 1967, the populace had rebelled, driven out the autocratic ruler – one General Pica by name – and introduced a radical democracy. Enthusiastically, *The Guardian* reported that the ensuing years had seen an economic upturn and the implementation of progressive social policies, while debates in the San Serriffe Parliament were no longer hamstrung by narrow party-political considerations.

KANTIA · CARIBBEAN SEA

Position 14th parallel north
Size uncertain
Sightings 1884
Maps uncertain

In 1884, the Leipzig merchant and avid yachtsman Johann Otto Polter was cruising around the Caribbean when he spotted an island looming out of the sea at the 14th parallel north. It lay a few nautical miles east of the outer arc of the Lesser Antilles and did not appear on any map. 'To the east, the Atlantic Ocean pounds with all its might against the rocky shoreline, kicking up plumes of spray. In the south and west, however, a calm turquoise sea laps gently over dazzling white sand. The north of the island is dominated by a mountain, whereas the south is somewhat flat – and everywhere the ground appears to be extremely fertile,' Polter noted, before continuing: 'The savages walk around as naked as the day they were born and are of impressive stature – they also seem to be well-disposed toward strangers. This is a paradise on Earth – and in honour of our greatest thinker I am christening it "Kantia."'

Four years later, in 1888, Polter set out to conduct a thorough investigation of the island. Intent on 'making this paradise part of our German homeland,' he financed the expedition from the considerable wealth that had accrued from his family's mercantile activities. The only problem was that the island failed to reappear. He tried again twice more, in 1903 and 1909, but to no avail. For as long as he lived, Polter refused to believe that he had been mistaken. Even in a photograph of him as a greying old man, he stares proudly into the distance, clutching in his left hand an official document identifying him as the discoverer of Kantia. At the bottom appear the words: 'On the service of His Majesty Wilhelm II, Emperor of the Germans and King of Prussia.' Kantia was a place of yearning for Germans, and Polter 'a fantastic sailor, in every sense of the word,' as the Swiss cultural commentator Samuel Herzog wrote in an article for the *Neue Zürcher Zeitung* on 22 May 2004. In this piece, Herzog speculated that Polter may have miscalculated the island's position. Then again, he may have been suffering from a bout of fever or the effects of an excess of rum.

Five years later, on 25 August 2009, the story was picked up by the Viennese newspaper *Der Standard*, which took the line that Polter must have been chasing after a phantom island. Soon after, a Wikipedia entry on the island appeared in German, followed by one in English. Thereafter, like so much flotsam, Kantia washed around in the comment pages of newspapers. In the German daily *Die Welt*, a reporter even claimed that the island 'had appeared on maps,' and so it was that Kantia slowly began to take on tangible form. Likewise, Antilia (see p. 12) had begun by just being a name on a map, before actually being depicted.

Kantia even made it into a monograph, which in turn had praise heaped upon it in a review in the *Süddeutsche Zeitung*. It was then mentioned in a variety of German media outlets, including *Deutschlandradio*, the *Ärzteblatt* (a weekly medical magazine), the *Rheinische Post*, the *Berliner Tagesspiegel*, *Die Zeit* and several more besides.

It is an incredible tale. And the most astonishing thing about it is that the entire thing is fictitious. It was the brainchild of Samuel Herzog, who invented the story after finding a shoebox at home full of old black-and-white photographs. Some of them showed people whom no one could remember. To try to get closer to them, Herzog invented all kinds of histories for them, including the whole tale about Polter and the island of Kantia. But with all these reports circulating, who can say for sure whether Kantia doesn't really exist somewhere out there?

KEENAN LAND · ARCTIC SEA

[KENNAN LAND]

Position north of Alaska
Size 520 square kilometres
Sightings during the 1870s
Maps Adolf Stieler (1891 and 1907)

RUSSIA

160°   170°

Towards the end of the 19th century, Captain John Keenan lost his bearings while sailing in Arctic waters. His aimless course took him across the Beaufort Sea, north of Alaska. Keenan had command of the 247-ton whaling barque *Stamboul*, whose home port was New Bedford in Massachusetts. His crew had already harpooned several whales when the weather turned. It is impossible to reconstruct with any certainty what happened next, given that the sources are so scanty and contradictory.

'They were heading north under light sail,' a seaman told the American naturalist Marcus Baker, co-founder of the National Geographic Society, in 1893. 'When the fog lifted, land was clearly visible to the north. All the men on board saw it. But because he was not engaged on a voyage of exploration and as no whales were in sight there, he was forced to sail farther south and continue his search there. The success of his trip depended on how many whales he caught.'

According to a more dramatic report, a storm blew up: the very first violent gust of wind smashed the *Stamboul*'s rudder to smithereens and broke the mast. For several days, the ship drifted northwards until it ran aground some 500 kilometres north of Alaska on an unknown shore. Keenan and his crew hoisted the Stars and Stripes at the highest point on the island, repaired their ship and subsequently informed the government in Washington D.C. about their discovery. Unfortunately, Keenan later mislaid his logbooks.

Throughout the 19th century, whalers told one another stories about mountains and islands in the Beaufort Sea. Geographers likewise took it for granted that there was land north of Alaska and believed that the permanent pack ice there never shifted because it was firmly anchored to the seabed. They even worked out the size of this land and sketched its probable position on maps. According to them, it was only a matter of time before the island was found.

German mapmakers also heard about Keenan's sighting, and in 1891, 'Kennan-Land' [sic] was shown on the map of the Arctic Sea in

Stielers Handatlas (*Stieler's Hand Atlas*), named after the cartographer Adolf Stieler; in the 1907 edition, the name of the island had been corrected to 'Keenan Land.'

A Canadian Arctic expedition spent the period from 1913 to 1916 exploring the region, but found no trace of the island. Similarly, in 1937, an aircraft scoured the Beaufort Sea on a search and rescue mission, but at no point sighted land.

It was a United States Air Force pilot and polar explorer by the name of Joseph O. Fletcher who finally solved the mystery of Keenan Land. During a flight over the Beaufort Sea in 1946, he registered an unusual radar signal. All of a sudden, he saw below him a gigantic island of ice with steep valleys and hills. Fletcher spent the next few hours crossing this terrain – a floating tabular iceberg visible only from the air – which, he estimated, covered an area of some 520 square kilometres. By contrast, at ground level, it was scarcely visible as an island; from a distance, all that could be seen were its mountains and valleys. Boulders and other debris that the iceberg had scraped off headlands on its journey made it look like land. Immense islands of ice like this regularly drift around with the ocean currents unnoticed for years on end.

KOREA · PACIFIC OCEAN

[COORAY, INSULA DE CORE, YLHAS DE CORE]

Position 37° 30' 0" North, 127° 0' 0" East
Size 220,000 square kilometres
Sightings c.1585
Maps Jan Huygen van Linschoten (1596)

KOREA

CHINA

JAPAN

Ladrone Island

Nobody noticed the spy in their midst. Although Jan Huygen van Linschoten was a Dutchman, he had long been working as a merchant in Barcelona and spoke both Spanish and Portuguese fluently. In 1583, he embarked for India to take up a post as secretary to the Portuguese Archbishop of Goa. In this capacity, various letters would land on his desk that, by rights, no Dutchman should ever have laid eyes upon.

For a long time, the Dutch had sourced their goods from Portugal, but three years before, Portugal had fallen under occupation by Spain. All foreign ships that tied up in the port of Lisbon were impounded, and ever since then, the Netherlands had been cut off from the spice trade.

In Goa, Linschoten set about gathering all the information he could concerning trading activity and sea routes in the Far East for his native country. Soon, he began copying the secret maritime charts of the colonial powers in the region. This was dangerous work, since these routes were state secrets. On a journey to another port on the west coast of India, he made the acquaintance of a Dutch swashbuckler who would become one of his most important informants: Dirck Gerritzsoon Pomp, alias Dirck China. Pomp had travelled to China on board the Portuguese merchant ship *Santa Cruz* and from there went on to Japan, where in 1585 he became the first Dutchman ever to set foot in the country.

Back in Goa, Pomp provided his friend Linschoten with an exhaustive account of his adventures, regaling him with tales of the exotic countries he had visited and of an island called Korea. Although he had not personally been there, Jesuits in the Far East had told him all about it.

After just six years in India, Linschoten made his way back to the Netherlands – and almost perished en route. His ship had rounded the Cape of Good Hope and was heading north when it ran into a storm off the Azores, which almost sank it. For two years thereafter, Linschoten found himself marooned on the island of Terceira, where he spent his time going through his notes and helping to repair the damaged ship. Eventually, he returned to his homeland via Lisbon.

Linschoten's reports of his travels appeared in 1595. In them, he detailed the colonial powers' sea routes to the Far East and wrote about Japan: '...so stretches the coast [from Japan] again to the north, recedes after that inward, northwestward, from whence those from Japan trade with the Nation which is called Cooray, from which I have good, comprehensive and true information, as well as about the navigation to this Country, from the pilots who investigated the situation there and sailed there.'

Cooray is also mentioned in his second book *Itinerario* of 1596: 'A little above Japan, on 34 and 35 degrees, not far from the coast of China, is another large island called Insula de Core, about which hitherto there has been no certainty concerning its size, people, nor what trade there is there.' Later in the same book, he adds: '20 miles southeast of the Enseada de Nanquin [sic] [Yellow Sea] lie several islands and finally on the eastern side there is situated a very large, mountainous island.' It was 'inhabited by many people, who either go about on foot or ride on horseback.'

Linschoten had little more of detailed substance to report, and it seems he was not even sure whether Korea was an archipelago: 'These islands, which are known to the Portuguese as the Ylhas de Core, or the Islands of Core, have a small indentation to the northwest. Its waters are not very deep, but it serves as a harbour. It also contains a small island where the Lord of the country has his residency. Twenty-five miles southeast of the main island, in the Enseada de Nanquin, lies the Japanese island of Goto.'

The book was accompanied by a map. For the first time, his Dutch compatriots could see what the countries on the far side of the globe looked like: there were the outlines of Cambodia, India and various Chinese provinces. Settlements were marked along the coasts, exotic animals were shown cavorting in gigantic patches of forest, and on the high seas, ships engaged one another in battle while sea monsters lay in wait for their prey. In the upper left-hand corner of the map, the Japanese archipelago with its numerous islands can be seen stretched out parallel to the equator, rather than in its expected orientation of North–South.

West of Japan on the Linschoten map lies Korea, an elongated island that is only separated from the mainland of the Asian continent by a narrow channel. In any event, some areas shown in dotted lines indicate that Linschoten did not fully trust his sources. It is true that, from a distance, modern-day Korea could indeed be taken for an island: the Yalu and Tumen rivers have such broad estuaries that Korea almost appears to be separated from the mainland by a strait. It did not take long for mariners to realise Linschoten's mistake.

For many decades, no European managed to set foot on Korea. Korean warships patrolled the coast, and as late as 1622, the Dutch vessel *de Hond* was attacked with cannons, arrows and wooden spears and driven back out to sea. And yet, of all people, it was a Dutchman who was the first European to give a detailed account of Korea: in 1653, a ship belonging to the seafarer Hendrick Hamel sank off the Korean coast. He was captured, taken to Seoul and later transferred to the countryside. Hamel lived on the peninsula for 13 years before finally managing to make his escape. For 200 years, his memoirs were the only source of information on this reclusive Eastern empire.

MARIA THERESA REEF
SOUTH PACIFIC OCEAN

[TABER, TABOR]

Position 36° 50' South, 136° 39' West;
also 37° 0' South, 151° 13' West
Size uncertain
Sightings Asaph P. Taber (1843)
Maps uncertain

Marshall Island

Fiji

Society Islands

Tonga

Cook Islands

Kermadec Islands

NEW ZEALAND

Chatham Islands

Wachusett Reef

MARIA THERESA
REEF

On 26 July 1864, the stately yacht *Duncan* was returning to Glasgow from a long voyage. As an island came into view, the sailor on watch suddenly spotted a hammerhead shark swimming in the yacht's wake. The *Duncan*'s owner, Lord Edward Glenarvan, immediately ordered a hook and line to be cast into the water, baited with a large hunk of meat. A few moments later, the beast took the bait and was hauled on deck, where it was promptly despatched and gutted. In its stomach, the sailors found a mysterious bottle. It contained a message written in three languages, but it was so damaged by seawater, only parts of it could be deciphered: '7 July 1862 ... Three-master Britannia ... Glasgow ... turned turtle ... −gonia ... −austral ... on land ... two sailors ... Captain Gr− ... gone ... Contin gef ... horrible ... indi ... document thrown ... Longitude and 37° 11' Latitude ... bring them help ... lost.' A sure sign that the missing Captain Robert Grant might still be alive!

On his return, Lord Glenarvan lost no time in provisioning a ship and sailing to South America with the children of the missing seafarer on board. From there – following the indications in the note – they sailed on westward across the Pacific along the 37th parallel south. After several weeks, they came across an island – the Maria Theresa Reef – which, as they described it, was of volcanic origin and had an elevation of 100 metres above sea level at its highest point. And before long, they found the missing captain safe and sound.

This story was told by Jules Verne, who had himself crewed aboard a yacht plying the waters of the English Channel, the North Sea and the Mediterranean. He included it in his novel *Les enfants du capitaine Grant* (published in English as *In Search of the Castaway*) of 1867. The island, he noted at one point, had 'been known about for a long time.' And later in the novel, there is the following passage of dialogue: '"But the island of Tabor – why, surely that's the one called Maria Theresa!" – "Absolutely right, Mr Paganel," replied Harry Grant. "It appears as Maria Theresa on German and English maps, but as Tabor on French ones."'

On reading this work in the early 1980s, Bernhard Krauth, a German schoolboy who was a fan of the works of Jules Verne, was seized by the urge to find out more about this island – specifically, where it was located and who had first discovered it. He couldn't find it in his school atlas, but he did manage to pinpoint it on an old tin globe that wasn't much bigger than a child's ball. There, it was shown as Maria-Theresia Riff and was situated on the 37th parallel south in the South Pacific, not far from the Tuamotu Archipelago, which formed part of French Polynesia. Now Krauth's research began in earnest, and it was not long before he found the island on some much better maps: first the world map in *Mairs Geographischer Verlag*, then in *Knaurs Großes Weltatlas*, a licensed edition of the renowned *Times Atlas of the World*. On both these maps, however, it appeared farther to the east. It was possible, Krauth reasoned, that Verne had been working from the Paris Meridian rather than the Prime Meridian when he specified its position.

In 1983, Krauth wrote to the German Foreign Office in Bonn, after reading that it had a repository of 3,000 atlases. They didn't really know anything of use, but did at least send him a copy of a map on a large scale of 1:20,000,000 from a Russian atlas showing the island as a tiny pinprick.

His next port of call was the German Hydrographic Institute in Hamburg, which informed him that the latest British maritime charts no longer included any information on the reef. The institute was responsible for producing German nautical charts – but in this case it was wrong. It took the schoolboy no time at all to locate Maria Theresa Reef on the most recent British charts, yet there too it was shown farther to the east than before.

Finally, Krauth got hold of the address of the UK Hydrographic Office. They told him that the coordinates of the reef had been revised in 1983 and set at 36° 50' South, 136° 39' West. However, the very existence of the reef was in doubt. Enclosed was a communication that had been crucial in prompting the repositioning of the island.

The reef's existence could be traced back to a ship's logbook from the year 1843, kept by one Asaph P. Taber. Taber was captain of the American whaling vessel *Maria Theresa* and made an entry in the logbook in rather illegible handwriting that could either be read as 'saw waves breaking' or 'saw whales breaching.' The entry was dated 16 November 1843, and the position was noted as 37° South and 137° West. Months after the supposed sighting, the newspaper *New-Bedford Mercury* broke the story of the new island, but the captain's name was erroneously given as Tabor rather than Taber, and although the island was reported as being at 37° South, the other coordinate was hundreds of miles farther to the west. This announcement was later reprinted without correction in other newspapers. Before long, the first charts appeared showing a reef in this same incorrect position – sometimes with the name Maria Theresa and sometimes Tabor – such as a French map from this period, which Krauth only acquired in 2006. Presumably Jules Verne knew this map; indeed, only four years separate the date of the map and the publication of the French author's *Les enfants du capitaine Grant*.

To this day, the existence of the reef remains uncertain; even satellite images do not clarify the matter. Perhaps it has sunk and is lurking dangerously just beneath the surface of the water? But as long as it has not been conclusively proven not to exist, it continues to be shown on maritime charts. Bernhard Krauth would have loved to visit the island. Indeed, he spent almost 15 years at sea, latterly captaining vessels, and even regularly crossed the North Pacific. However, he never got close to the island in the South Pacific that had so fascinated him as a boy.

NEW SOUTH GREENLAND
SOUTHERN OCEAN

Position 62° 41' South, 47° 21' West (North Cape)

Size 480 kilometres long

Sightings 1821, 1823, 1843

Maps uncertain

Elephant Island

Clarence Island

South Orkney Islands

South Shetland Islands

Bransfield Strait

NEW SOUTH GREENLAND

James Ross Island

GRAHAM LAND

Robertson Island

60°

60°

50°

I t was mid-1912, and the German Antarctic research ship *Deutschland* found herself frozen fast in a vast area of pack ice in the Southern Ocean. Unable to manoeuvre, the ship could do nothing but drift with the ice in a northwesterly direction. The expedition leader Wilhelm Filchner followed this unplanned course daily on his charts. With every day that passed, the ship was getting closer and closer to the disputed island of New South Greenland.

On 23 June, when the ship was little more than 60 kilometres from the island, Filchner proposed striking out from the vessel on foot to try to find it. He didn't have much time at his disposal; the ice was still thick enough to walk on, but no one knew how long it would remain so. Above all, it was entirely possible that the huge ice floe could at any time start to turn imperceptibly, meaning that he might never be able to locate the ship again. To accompany him on this excursion, Filchner had approached Alfred Kling and a researcher called Felix König, both of whom had cheerfully and unsuspectingly jumped at the opportunity. Kling was an expert navigator and König, as a former Alpine mountaineer, knew his way around all kinds of ice.

Prior to their departure, Filchner left very precise instructions with the captain about possible rescue measures: from the fourth day onwards, he was to hang a navigation lamp every night from the mainmast, and from the seventh day on, a signal rocket was to be let off at six o'clock sharp every evening. After two weeks, a rescue party was to be sent out and black flags were to be hoisted on the highest points of the pack ice.

And so, on that Sunday in late June, Filchner, König and Kling sped off in a westerly direction on their dog sleds. It was -35°C, and they had sufficient provision with them for two weeks.

The island had first been described almost 90 years before by Benjamin Morrell – the same sea Captain who had sighted Byers and Morrell Islands (see p. 46) in the Pacific. 'At half past 4 p.m. we were close in with the eastern coast of the body of land to which Captain Johnson had given the name New South Greenland,' he noted on 15 March 1823. The next day his ship was cruising 'about two miles from the land.' Morrell could make out snow-covered mountains. Yet despite the fact that it abounded 'with oceanic birds of every description... three thousand sea-elephants, and one hundred and fifty sea-dogs and leopards [that is, elephant seals, seals and leopard seals],' it still struck him as an 'Island of Desolation.' On the fourth day, Morrell passed the island's northern tip, whose position he determined as being latitude 62° 41' South and longitude 47° 21' West.

It proved to be an arduous first day for Filchner, König and Kling. The southern hemisphere was in the grip of winter, and so close to the South Pole, the sun did not climb above the horizon at this time of year. Even so, its light still enabled the three men to get their bearings in the polar night. After travelling just a few hundred metres, they avoided a hole in the ice and changed their course to head northwest. Time and again, their sleds got stuck in the pack ice.

The dogs, which were hitched to the sleds in packs of eight, kept on getting tangled up in the traces, so that the harnesses had to be repeatedly untied. 'It's the most unpleasant task on dog sled trips,' Kling complained in his account of the expedition; the work had to be carried out with bare hands in sub-zero temperatures – plus he had to keep an eagle eye on the dogs in case they made a run for it.

At two o'clock in the afternoon, darkness began to fall. The men quickly unloaded the sleds, erected a tent and tied the dogs securely to the sleds. Each animal was given a strict ration of two pounds of dried cod to eat. In the tent, the men melted snow on their portable stove and rubbed the icicles out of their beards. Even under canvas, it was so cold that their ungloved fingers instantly stuck to every bit of exposed metal. They ate some crispbread and a portion of hard-frozen sausage. With the aid of a marlinspike, they were able to hack off small pieces and chew them. They conversed in a feverish fashion, trying to ward off any thoughts of the roast meat and wine that was customarily served on board the ship every Sunday. 'Today, we had only managed six kilometres; we were certain that we would never be able to carry out our task if the pack ice continued to be so impassable,' noted Kling.

Icicles grew in their beards overnight. When they arose at around nine o'clock the next morning, they felt drained and their limbs ached. They brewed tea, ate biscuits and lashed the rolled-up tent to a sled. At around 11, they resumed their journey across the fissured pack ice. 'If one of us had fallen into the water, he would surely have perished before he had a chance to get into some dry clothes in this bitter weather,' Kling remarked. At one point, a fin whale surfaced through the ice, blew a spout of water high into the air and submerged once more. 'We stared transfixed at the spot where it had broken through, unable to utter a word; in that moment we were all thinking the same thought – what would have happened if we'd been standing directly above it?' In the ghostly half-light, the whole thing seemed like a hallucination.

By that second afternoon, they had only covered another four kilometres. In the tent, they sat around the stove despondently. The ice was proving more difficult to overcome than anticipated. No one spoke, and before long, they crept into their sleeping bags and prayed that a crevasse wouldn't open up beneath them as they slept. In a few hours' time it would be Kling's birthday: he lay there in his sleeping bag thinking about the years gone by, 'when suddenly there came to my lips unbidden the following rhyme: "I'm thirty soon, and in that time / Have passed through storms and hail / But on this ice I see ahead / Just sorrow and travail."'*

On the third day, 25 June, Kling woke in the dark but to his astonishment found that it was already nine o'clock in the morning. He

---

*Kling's rhyme is a wry adaptation of a well-known German soldiers' song *Der Alte Mantel* (*The old overcoat*), which was composed in the 1820s.

roused his comrades, who wished him the compliments of the day. Even in the midst of this icy waste he felt like celebrating his birthday: 'I've brought with me my two best cigars, which I fully intend to smoke today.' They only broke camp at half past ten and spent an hour travelling southwest over pack ice when they suddenly encountered sheet ice. Their onward journey west now proceeded apace. When Kling attempted to determine their position, however, he found the compass had frozen solid. He buried it deep within the folds of his clothes to thaw out the sensitive glycerine inside, but after 90 minutes the needle still refused to budge. Their rangefinder wasn't working either, forcing them to navigate by the moon. 'Our situation appears pretty alarming,' Kling confided to his journal. How would they find out where they were or manage to make their way back to the ship if the massive ice floe on which they found themselves kept constantly shifting position?

But at least they had covered 18 kilometres that day. Elated at this, they sat and chatted animatedly around the humming stove. They even succeeded in mending the compass.

The dogs started barking wildly, but the men stayed put inside their sleeping bags. At 11 in the morning, the moon emerged from behind a bank of cloud – to reveal that the dogs had bolted, taking the sleds with them! A loud howling could be heard in the distance. Kling grabbed a whip and chased after the dogs. In a gully, he found the animals fighting with a seal. He laid into the dogs with his whip, but they only ceased their attack momentarily; they didn't calm down until Kling had despatched the wounded animal with an ice pick.

The next morning, Kling was in command of the lead sled, giving the dog team directions through blasts on a whistle: one blast meant 'more to the right,' two blasts 'more to the left' and three blasts 'stop.' Finally, the ice conditions were good. They kept moving until three in the afternoon, by which time they had covered 25 kilometres that day, putting them 53 kilometres in total away from the ship. To ascertain their position, Kling put up a theodolite – a device for measuring angles. In temperatures of -30 °C, he carefully turned the small calibration wheel with his bare fingers. First, he tried taking a sighting on the star Sirius, but his fingers froze onto the metal telescope of the device. Filchner took over from him. They found they could only work at the theodolite for a few seconds at a time before putting their gloves back on and waving their arms about to get their circulation going again.

Finally, Sirius became visible as a tiny point of light. They had brought an electric torch with them in order to see the readings on the dial, but it refused to work in the extreme cold. Instead, they had to make do with a lantern containing a candle. After two hours, they had finally determined all the coordinates. In ordinary circumstances this task would have taken them no longer than 10 minutes.

Over a cup of tea in the tent, Kling calculated their position as being latitude 70° 32' South and longitude 43° 45' West. This was an extraordinary finding that simply didn't tally, but Kling assured his companions that he would be able to find the ship again. They agreed to go on for just one more day and then turn back. It was so cold that a thin layer of hoarfrost formed on the inside of the tent. Even the insides of their nostrils froze. 'I'm astonished that we made it back on board with our noses intact,' Kling wrote later. 'I had taken some reasonable precautions against the effects of frostbite by tying a handkerchief round the lower part of my face at night; every morning, I found it had frozen stiff as a board.'

The following morning, they steered their way around a wide hole in the ice. After several kilometres, when there was still no end to the icy waste in sight, Filchner decided to take a sounding of the ocean bed. By now, they were at roughly the same point as where Morrell had sighted land from his ship. A sled was pushed to the edge of an ice hole, and on it they fashioned a rudimentary winch with a plumb line by feeding an iron bar through the middle of a reel of wire and securing it to the front of the sled. For a brake, they used a snowshoe, one end of which rested against the wire reel while the other was anchored to the sled. A 75-pound lump of iron served as a plumb bob.

Kling sat at the front of the sled and held some pliers loosely around the wire so he could tell when the plummet touched the sea floor. After a few hundred metres, the layers of wire became tangled and kinks started to appear. Clearly, the wire had been wound too loosely onto the drum. At 1,200 metres the wire snapped. 'At least by taking this sounding we had fulfilled our task, since the land that we'd been promised was there could neither be seen, nor could there possibly be any land in the vicinity according to our sounding,' wrote Kling. They had travelled 57 kilometres from the *Deutschland*; by rights, it should have been only eight kilometres further to New South Greenland. Indeed, because of the effect of ocean drift on the ice floe, they had actually travelled 102 kilometres from their starting point. Morrell must have been mistaken.

Three years after this second German Antarctic expedition, the British explorer Ernest Shackleton would confirm their observation when he found himself likewise icebound close to the supposed location of New South Greenland. 'I decided that Morrell Land must be added to the long list of Antarctic islands and continental coasts that have resolved themselves into icebergs,' he wrote on 17 August 1915. Three days later, Shackleton witnessed a mirage of the Fata Morgana type: 'The distant pack is thrown up into towering barrier-like cliffs, which are reflected in blue lakes and lanes of water at their base. Great white and golden cities of Oriental appearance at close intervals along these clifftops indicate distant bergs, some not previously known to us.'

By the time the three German researchers completed their sounding and set off, it was already dark. In the twilight, they kept losing the sled tracks they had made on their outward journey. Finally, they found the place where they had pitched camp the previous night. By now, Kling was fearful that they might not be able to find the *Deutschland* again after all.

The day of 28 June was foggy. In two days' time, there would be a full moon, and that spelt danger, because the tides it would generate would make it more likely that the ice floe would break apart and shift in a totally unpredictable way. Using their old tracks as a guide, they steered their way back towards the ship. During their return journey, the hungry dogs suddenly gave chase to three plump seals and could not be reined in. The expedition lost a precious hour and found it impossible to locate their old trail again. They set a course bearing east by northeast. Kling wanted to keep on this bearing until they encountered the pack ice again. If he couldn't see the ship from that point, he would try heading directly northeast instead. At some stage, they would surely catch sight of two distinctively shaped icebergs that were about 15 kilometres away from the ship. In the fog, they made swift progress across the smooth ice field. After three kilometres, they duly picked up their old tracks once more.

As darkness fell, the fog lifted, and they resolved to press on in the pale moonlight. 'We sped along soundlessly, as though we were making for Valhalla,' mused Kling. 'Around us, everything was as quiet as the grave; the demonic silence was only broken by the monotonous creaking of the sleds and the sound of König shouting commands to the dogs.' All of a sudden, a whale emerged from an ice hole and blew a fountain of spray skywards. They could scarcely read the compass in the poor light. Kling navigated initially by the moon and later by the position of the planets: 'An astrologer once told me that Jupiter was my lucky star, and so I found myself involuntarily gazing up reverentially at the planet and uttering a heartfelt plea not to let us down in our hour of need.'

Presently, they came to a huge water hole two kilometres across and covered with a sheet of ice no thicker than a hand's breadth. This was the most dangerous obstacle on their entire journey. König put on snowshoes and tried to find a way across. When he waved back, the rest of the party picked their way gingerly ahead; even the dogs stretched out their paws and tested the ice ahead with each step before proceeding. Halfway across, small fissures suddenly began to appear.

The ice sheet bowed beneath their every step, and water bubbled up and flowed over the dark, glassy surface of the ice.

They only breathed more easily when they finally felt firm ground beneath their feet once more. Soon, they reached the pack ice, which made the going more difficult again. At around half past eight, the exhausted dogs refused to go any further, so the men made camp. They had covered no less than 34 kilometres that day!

On 29 June, the day dawned clear and bright. Kling climbed up a hill of ice and spotted a ship's mast on the horizon. At first, however, he said nothing; some days previously, all three men had been fooled by mirages. But when they looked through binoculars, they could clearly see that it was the *Deutschland*, approximately 16 kilometres away. They might even make it back on board before nightfall.

Soon after, the men found themselves standing once more in front of an immense ice hole; there appeared to be no way of crossing it. Just at that moment, they heard shouts – from the far side, they could see their comrades waving to them. Initially they could do nothing to help, so the three companions were forced to spend one last night camping on the ice. To celebrate their imminent homecoming, they cooked themselves a pea soup with sausage and half a tin of corned beef. Kling remarked: 'I cannot recall food ever tasting so good.'

In the morning, they heard the sound of cracking ice and assumed that the ice hole was closing up. But when the day dawned, it turned out that there was still open water in the middle of it. Eventually, their comrades from the ship reappeared and, one after the other, ferried the three men, their dogs and their sleds in a rowing boat across to the far side.

On the ship, they saw a lantern alight high up on the mainmast. Their shipmates told them how the *Deutschland* had been driven back and forth in a zigzag pattern: first to the southwest, then northwest and back to the east in between. In their cabins, everything seemed as strange and alien to them as if they had been living in the wilderness for years. Their fur coats felt like suits of armour and the pain in their fingertips was excruciating. Five days after his birthday, Kling celebrated the occasion anew, this time with wine, music and singing. All those present joined in, though there was one notable absence: Wilhelm Filchner was confined to his bunk, suffering from heart spasms.

SOUTH AMERICA

Patagonia

Strait of Magel

Tierra del Fuego

Cape Horn

PEPYS ISLAND

Falkland Islands

Staten Island

PEPYS ISLAND
SOUTH ATLANTIC

Position 47° South
Size uncertain
Sightings William Ambrosia Cowley (1683)
Maps uncertain

In late 1683, the British seafarer William Ambrosia Cowley was lost in the South Atlantic. Cowley was a buccaneer, one of the loose coalition of privateers who styled themselves the 'Brethren of the Coast.' The French, Dutch and Spanish saw him as nothing more than a pirate, but Cowley was a cut above your common cutthroat: he had his own ship and crew and even counted several politicians in London among his friends. Where the British were concerned, buccaneers were low-cost mercenaries who helped plunder the vessels of rival nations. The monarchy had long since legalised the practice of privateering, and even took a cut of the spoils. The buccaneers were based at Port Royal in Jamaica, from where they sallied forth to attack and loot coastal settlements around the Caribbean.

Cowley's command – the *Bachelor's Delight* – was armed with 40 guns. As the vessel sailed southwest along the 47th parallel south, Cowley sighted an unknown and uninhabited island. He named it Pepys Island after his friend and secretary to the Admiralty Samuel Pepys, who later became celebrated as a diarist. Cowley's logbook contains the following entry: 'We found it a very commodious place for Ships to water at and take in Wood, and it has a very good Harbour, where a thousand sail of Ships may safely ride: Here is great plenty of Fowls, and we judge, abundance of Fish, by reason of the Grounds being nothing but Rocks and Sands.' Pepys Island also provided the buccaneers with a perfect base from which to patrol the sea lanes to South America and launch raids on coastal towns. It would be a long time before anyone found their hideout on this remote island.

In January 1684, Cowley fleshed out his observations on Pepys Island in his logbook: 'In this month we arrived at latitude 47° 40' S and noticed an island to our west with the wind ENE. We headed towards it but as it was late to approach the coast spent the night off the cape. The island had a pleasant aspect, there were woods, one might say it was totally wooded. To the east of the island was a rock on which there were a number of birds the size of small ducks. Our crew hunted them as our ship passed by and killed as many as we needed for food, they were quite tasty but spoiled by their fishy flavour.' In the afternoon of the same day he made his discovery, Cowley sighted another island which he thought might be one of the Sebaldes, as some of the outlying western islands of the Falklands were then known. He also drew a sketch of the islands and the straits.

In 1764, the British government sent Patrick Mouat and John Byron on a secret mission to the South Atlantic to map the region and search for Pepys Island. From Rio de Janeiro, they set sail eastward along the 47th parallel. They reckoned that the Aurora Islands (see p. 20) must also lie somewhere hereabouts. A botanist on the voyage reported that the lookout had on one occasion spotted something looking like an island, but the supposed island grew no larger as they approached it.

Having failed in their attempt to find Pepys Island, Mouat and Byron set a course for the Falkland Islands, which lay three degrees of latitude farther south than Pepys. There, they ascertained that Cowley's sketch, including the strait he had pictured, corresponded in certain key details to the Falkland Islands. It seems that the buccaneer had in fact been the first to sight the island group that Byron duly claimed for the British crown and over which the United Kingdom has maintained sovereignty – through the exercise of military force when necessary – to the present day.

Isle Royale

PHÉLIPEAUX

Apostle Islands

PHÉLIPEAUX AND PONTCHARTRAIN
LAKE SUPERIOR

[PHILIPPAUX]

Position **uncertain**
Size **uncertain**
Sightings **uncertain**
Maps **Jacques-Nicolas Bellin (1744), John Mitchell (1755)**

49°

Michipicoten Island

PONTCHARTRAIN

48°

Hocquart Island

St. Anne Island

47°

In the summer of 1782, a team of negotiators from the United States arrived in France. Headed by Benjamin Franklin, its aim was to bring the war for independence against the British motherland to an end and settle the borders in North America. The negotiations were difficult. Only a handful of European men had ever explored the new nation's woods, lakes and rivers, and hardly any region was more remote than the environs of the Great Lakes, though fur trappers would occasionally venture there from Montreal or Hudson Bay. The whole of eastern North America had been mapped in 1755 by John Mitchell, who was actually a doctor by trade. Time and again, the negotiators returned to pore over this map, which measured 2 metres wide by 1.4 metres high and was fascinatingly accurate in many of its details.

In Paris, the wrangling continued over fishing rights, reparations payments and the return of land that had been expropriated. It took months for the two sides to agree the finer details of the border between the United States and the British colonies in Canada. In Lake Superior, it was resolved that the frontier should henceforth weave between three islands: Isle Royal and the supposedly mineral-rich Phélipeaux would in future belong to the United States, while the island of Pontchartrain would become part of the British colony of Canada. In paragraph IV of the peace accord, it was stipulated that the northwestern border should run 'through Lake Superior northward of the Isles Royal and Phélipeaux to the Long Lake; thence through the middle of said Long Lake and the water communication between it and the Lake of the Woods, to the said Lake of the Woods; thence through the said Lake to the most northwesternmost point thereof.' The agreement was concluded on 3 September 1783. As the representative of the British monarch King George III, David Hartley the Younger placed his signature beneath the Treaty of Paris, while Benjamin Franklin, John Adams and John Jay signed on behalf of the United States. The American War of Independence had formally came to an end, and the United States was finally a sovereign state.

In the early years of the 19th century, an American government commission was appointed to survey the last uncharted stretches of the border with Canada running through the dense forests and valleys of this region. The head of the commission, General Peter Buell Porter, offered the following laconic summary: 'A totally wild & uninhabited country, affording no means for the comfort or even subsistence of persons engaged in this service, and a climate so cold and inhospitable that a small portion only of the year can be employed in active duties.' The general said nothing about Phélipeaux, however.

In February 1824, the board of commissioners met in Albany, capital of the American state of New York, to finally determine the United States–Canada frontier though the Great Lakes. A report that was submitted spoke of 13 'considerable' rivers that supposedly emptied into Lake Superior along its northern shore and proposed further investigation of these. But even at this stage it was becoming clear, the commissioners concluded, that several points of reference in the Treaty of Paris had proved to be incorrect or at least doubtful. For instance, the island of Phélipeaux definitely did not exist. Likewise, the Canadians were subsequently to search in vain for the island of Pontchartrain.

Over time, it transpired that the cartographer John Mitchell had used earlier French maps as his model when drawing up his map of the eastern United States. The islands were originally on a map prepared by the Parisian geographer Jacques-Nicolas Bellin in 1744. While Isle Royal incontestably did exist, Bellin had simply invented the islands of Phélipeaux and Pontchartrain, naming them in honour of his former patron, Louis II Phélypeaux, Count of Pontchartrain (1643–1727), a minister of the 'Sun King', Louis XIV.

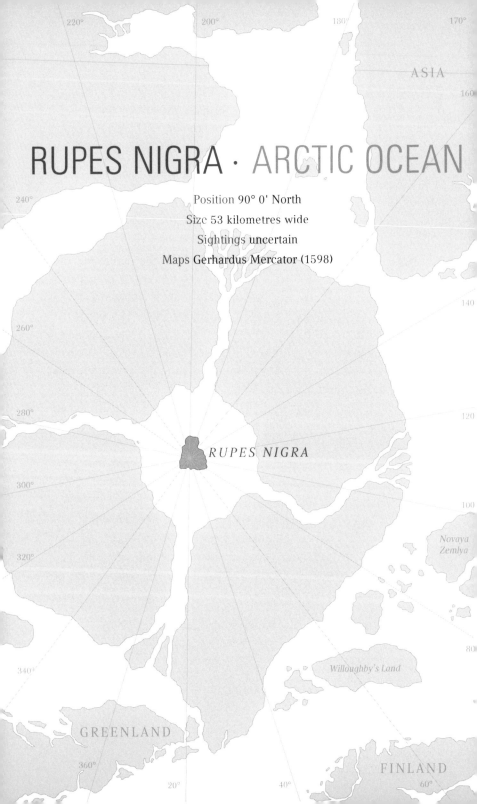

RUPES NIGRA · ARCTIC OCEAN

Position 90° 0' North
Size 53 kilometres wide
Sightings uncertain
Maps Gerhardus Mercator (1598)

RUPES NIGRA

According to a Franciscan friar from Oxford, in the mid-14th century an army under a British ruler named King Arthur conquered the islands north of Norway. In these extreme latitudes, the sun hardly rose for months on end, and it was bitterly cold and dark. The mountains soared into the clouds. Between the islands, the sea flowed in the direction of the North Pole. The ocean currents were so strong that no ship could make headway against them, not even with the assistance of a violent storm with a following wind. Almost 4,000 people had pitted themselves against these currents and never returned. On just one occasion, eight men managed to extricate themselves from the raging torrents and make it to the court of the Norwegian king. Among their number was the Franciscan friar, who recounted their tale in his book *Inventio Fortunata*. Yet, in truth, there wasn't even a king by the name of Arthur on the throne at that time.

No cartographer worked more meticulously or consulted more sources than the Flemish mapmaker Gerardus Mercator, who lived in Duisburg, Germany for the last 30 years of his life. While preparing a map of the North Pole region in the mid-16th century, he read the *Inventio Fortunata* along with a work called the *Itinerarium* (*Travel Report*) by a Brabantian traveller called Jacobus Cnoyen of 's-Hertogenbosch, which contained a reference to an earlier historical volume, the *Res gestae Arturi Britanni* (*The Heroic Deeds of Arthur of Britain*). All three works were later lost; we only know about them thanks to Mercator's reference to them. In the Arctic Ocean, Mercator explained, his research indicated that there were four large islands surrounding the North Pole. At their centre was a mighty whirlpool, where the water thundered around incessantly in a circle before flowing into the bowels of the Earth beneath the Pole. Located directly over the Pole, however, was a patch of land in the middle of the maelstrom which took the form of a bare mountain. In a letter, Mercator called this island Rupes Nigra – 'Black Rock' – and described it thus: 'Its circumference is almost 33 French miles and it is all of magnetic stone.' The island, black and shining, rose sheer into the clouds, 'and nothing grows on it, for there is no more than a handful of soil on it.'

Ever since the maritime compass had been invented in the 12th century, geographers had speculated that there must be some such lodestone mountain. If a ship sailed too close to it, it was said, the nails would be dragged from the vessel's timbers by the magnetic force. Martin Behaim had included land at this location on his 1492 Erdapfel – the world's first terrestrial globe – though at this stage it did not take the form of a magnetic mountain, but a pair of islands just west of the North Pole. To the east of this, Northern Europe and Asia formed a semi-circular body of land. Not long after, in 1508, Johannes Ruysch depicted four islands at this spot on his map of the world and reported that the channels of water rushing between them were drawn in an enormous whirlpool down into the core of the earth.

Norse mythology had long spoken of a spring called Hvergelmir, which was thought to feed all the rivers of the world. It was said that the water flowed in and out through subterranean channels and that this was visible at the coast in the ebb and flow of the tides. 'Not far from the coast of which I spoke previously, in the West where the sea spreads out boundlessly, is that very deep abyss of the waters we commonly call the Ocean's Navel,' wrote the 8th-century author Paul the Deacon. Ships were believed to be drawn into the whirlpool so forcibly that they flew as fast as arrows through the air; at the last moment, though, many were swept back out by a sudden upwelling and backwash.

Mercator took in all this information when preparing his atlas. And although Rupes Nigra finally disappeared from maps not long after, the theory of a swirling maelstrom persisted. As a result, as late as the 19th century, some researchers and seafarers still believed that the Arctic Ocean was free of ice.

TRIVIA

The satirist Jonathan Swift (1667–1745) was inspired by the story of the magnetic mountain. 'The reader can hardly conceive my astonishment, to behold an island in the air, inhabited by men, who were able [...] to raise or sink, or put it into progressive motion, as they pleased,' recounts Lemuel Gulliver, hero of Swift's most famous work, *Gulliver's Travels*, which was published in 1726. The island, called Laputa, is circular. In its centre is a powerful magnet that provides the island with its motive force. However, Laputa turns out to be anything but a paradise; the Laputians are in a state of perpetual disquietude, Gulliver reports, never enjoying a minute's peace of mind, and they talk incessantly without ever understanding one another.

Azores

SAINT BRENDAN'S ISLANDS
ATLANTIC OCEAN

Position near the Canary Islands

Size uncertain

Sightings c.530, 1719, 1721, 1759

Maps Ebstorf Mappa Mundi (1235),

Angelino Dulcert (1339), Martin Behaim (1492)

Porto Santo

Madeira

Canary Islands

La Palma　　*Tenerife*

SAINT BRENDAN'S ISLANDS　　*El Hierro*

Gran Canaria　　*Fuerteventura*

35°

30°

25°

AFRICA

20°

Cape Verde Islands

The Irish abbot Saint Brendan fasted for 40 days before setting sail on the Atlantic in the company of 14 monks, on a voyage to look for the legendary Isle of the Blessed. Their boat was made of wood covered with the stretched hides of oxen. After 40 days at sea, they sighted their first island. It was so precipitous and rocky that they spent three days searching for a safe spot where they could drop anchor. Once on dry land, they came across a great hall with a table laid for a banquet. Brendan warned his companions not to let themselves be seduced by Satan into helping themselves to any of the food, but one of the monks stole something all the same. No prayers were able to save him, and his soul was taken by Lucifer.

Brendan and the other monks travelled on from one island to the next. They once came across huge sheep, and on another occasion, they drank from a magic spring whereupon some of them fell into a deep sleep lasting three days and three nights. On an even more distant island, they encountered a tree full of white birds. One bird flew down and informed Brendan that they would have to sail on for another seven years before they reached the Promised Land of the Saints.

Later, the travellers came to an island that was full of purple fruit. At another spot, the air smelt of pomegranates. One time, they even saw a forge belching out dense smoke and heard the ringing of heavy hammer blows. On another island, they lit a fire using driftwood, but when the island suddenly began to sink, they fled back to their ship and realised that they had been camped on the back of a whale.

So they sailed from island to island. The story recounts how the sea once began to curdle and, on another occasion, started boiling, after which there wasn't a breath of wind for weeks on end. At one point, a sea monster attacked the monks without warning and tried to devour them. They prayed until a fire-breathing dragon appeared and cut the monster into three pieces. Later, a griffin swooped down on them; once again, God sent a huge bird to rescue them. Angels told them on which islands they were to spend Easter, Whitsun and Christmas. Once, they saw the traitor Judas Iscariot sitting on a rocky outcrop.

Elsewhere, they got to know a hermit who lived on a diet of fish and drank fresh water from a spring that only flowed on Sundays. He was awaiting the Day of Judgement and gave Brendan his blessing. From there, they sailed eastwards for 40 days. When they finally arrived off the island of their yearnings, they found it shrouded in dense fog. Landing on the beach there, they were embraced by a young man who confirmed that they had reached the Isle of the Blessed. God kept his secrets in the great ocean, the youth told them. They only remained a short time on the island, gathering fruit and precious stones before heading back to their homeland.

Abbot Brendan was a real historical figure: he was born in around AD 480 in the southwest of Ireland and was ordained a priest in AD 512. After gathering a number of followers around him, he founded a monastery, and travelled to the Hebrides, Orkney and the Faroe Islands. It was said of so-called 'Brendan the Navigator' that he went in search of the Promised Land. The story of his epic journey first appeared in the early 9th century. Over time, no fewer than 120 different manuscripts were written about his exploits in Latin alone, not to mention the other accounts that were subsequently written in Irish Gaelic, Flemish, Catalan, German, French, Norwegian and Anglo-Norman.

Saint Brendan's Islands were first depicted on a mappa mundi of 1235, which forms the altarpiece at the Benedictine monastery at Ebstorf in Lower Saxony. The map is circular and shows a labyrinth of rivers, cities and seas, as well as scenes from the Bible and animals. At its centre stands Jerusalem, while at its far edge an island can be seen, beside it the following inscription: '*Insula perdita: hanc invenit Sanctus Brandanus a qua cum navigasset a nullo hominum postea est inventa*' ('The lost island: this is the island that Saint Brendan sighted and that no man ever saw again thereafter'). The island is shown at a point where the Atlas Mountains border on the Atlantic Ocean – roughly the same latitude as the Canary Islands. Gervase of Tilbury, the provost of Ebstorf Abbey, is widely thought to be the map's creator.

Gervase was also the author of an encyclopedic work called the *Otia Imperialia* – also known as the *Book of Marvels* – a compendium of learning in history, geography and physics. One of the sources for this manuscript was the work *Imago Mundi* by Honorius Augustodunensis of Regensburg, an encyclopedia of popular cosmology and geography dating from around 1100. In it, Honorius recounted tales of the Island of the Gorgons, the Hesperides and Perdita (or the 'Lost Island'). According to the legend, Perdita could never be found through purposeful searching, but only by chance. This paradise 'far exceeded all the surrounding countries in the delightfulness and fertility of all things to be found therein,' he wrote.

At the beginning of the 14th century, Europeans started to colonise the Canary Islands, which thereby lost the allure of the unknown. On the portolan chart prepared by the Italian-Majorcan Angelino Dulcert in 1339, Saint Brendan's Islands migrated farther to the north. Three islands named Canaria, Insula de Caprara and Coruimaris are grouped under the umbrella term *Insulle Sct Brandani sive puellarum*: the islands of St. Brendan. It is clear that these depict the islands we now know as Madeira. Henceforth, on sea charts, Saint Brendan's Islands kept shifting ever farther westward to the farthest extremity of the known world at any given time.

Nonetheless, expeditions continued to search for them west of Africa. Lists of supposed eyewitnesses were even drawn up. In 1759, a Franciscan friar wrote in a letter that he had long yearned to see the Island of San Borondon one day; from La Palma, at six o'clock on the morning of 3 May and in conditions of clear visibility, he reported seeing not only the island of El Hierro, but another island farther in the distance. Looking through a telescope, he could see that its centre was covered with dense forest. The friar claimed that a crowd of 40 people had spent an hour and a half observing the island, though by midday, it had disappeared.

The strong currents that flow between the Canary Islands only add to the confusion. In his *Noticias* of 1772, the chronicler José de Viera y Clavijo told the story of a Canarian sea captain who was returning from the Americas with his flotilla. He thought he had already sighted La Palma, 'but when he duly set course for Tenerife, he was astonished to see the real La Palma suddenly materialise off his bows the following morning.' A similar entry can be found in the diaries of Colonel Don Roberto de Rivas. One afternoon, his ship was nearing the island of La Palma, but he only arrived there late the following day. The winds and currents, he concluded, must have been extremely adverse overnight.

With the discovery of the Americas, Saint Brendan's Islands found themselves pushed right to the far western edge of the Atlantic. At that point, only a single island had appeared on maps for a long time: in the 16th century, Abraham Ortelius sited the island of 'San Brandani' off Newfoundland, north of Frisland (see p. 66). After 1,300 years, it finally ended up stranded in a group of islands deep in Bonavista Bay off the Newfoundland coast; in 1884 this island was rechristened Cottel Island (which has a small settlement called St Brendan's).

TRIVIA

In 1976, the British historian and explorer Tim Severin retraced the journey of Saint Brendan. Together with four companions, he set sail across the Atlantic in a traditional currach made of timber and tanned ox hides, a replica of the boat used by Brendan. In doing so, he proved that Brendan could well have reached America. If this were indeed the case, the Irish cleric would have been the first European to set foot in the New World, some 400 years before the Vikings landed at L'Anse aux Meadows on Newfoundland.

SANDY ISLAND
EASTERN CORAL SEA, PACIFIC OCEAN

[ÎLE DE SABLE, SABLE ISLAND]

Position 19° 13' 6.4" South, 159° 55' 23.4" East
Size 120 square kilometres
Sightings 1876
Maps *National Geographic*, Google Earth, and others

SANDY ISLAND

Cook Reefs

French Reefs

20°

Minerva Shoals

Bellona Shoals

Fairway Reef

NEW CALEDON[

South Bellona Reef

160°

What a nightmare if the ship were to hit a reef! Or run aground on shallows, or be shipwrecked in the middle of the eastern Coral Sea, 100 kilometres from the nearest island of New Caledonia and a full 1,100 kilometres from the vessel's home port of Brisbane in Australia. Yet from the deck of the *Southern Surveyor*, right up to the horizon, there had been nothing to see for hours but open sea. And according to the measuring instruments on board, they weren't in any danger: the ocean here was 1,300 metres deep, with nothing to suggest any shoals hereabouts, let alone an island.

Even so, Captain Fred Stein was feeling nervous in a way that was rare for him during his career at sea. On the meteorological charts that he was relying upon, an island was definitely marked at this point – likewise in the maps drawn up by the National Geographic Society and even on the satellite images on Google Earth. There, at the coordinates 19° 14' South, 159° 56' East, a pixellated black bar could be seen, like a barrier in the ocean: a piece of land named Sandy Island, some 24 kilometres long and 5 kilometres wide. If it really did exist, and the captain was in no doubt that it did, it would be almost twice the size of Manhattan – an island, in other words, that really couldn't be ignored.

Stein gave the order to proceed ahead slowly. Metre by metre, the research ship ploughed its way through the sea. At the ship's bows, more than 20 scientists – who had all been ordered up on deck – scanned the water. They stared intently, straining to see if even the sea floor became visible or if any waves were breaking, which would indicate the presence of a dangerous reef located just beneath the surface.

It was mid-November 2012, and for just over three weeks, scientists from the University of Sydney had been surveying the eastern Coral Sea. The expedition was being led by Maria Seton, a 33-year-old marine geologist. Her brief was to investigate the geological history of the fifth continent. During the Archean geologic eon, Australia, India, South America, Madagascar, the Arabian Peninsula and Antarctica all formed the gigantic landmass known as Gondwana. Over time, this supercontinent broke into pieces. Eventually, around 45 million years ago, Australia and Antarctica also separated from one another. In studying the far eastern edge of the Indo-Australian tectonic plate, the researchers on board the *Southern Surveyor* charted 14,000 square kilometres of the ocean floor and took almost 200 rock and soil samples.

Day by day, Seton had followed the ship's course on the navigational charts. Now and then, she corrected the course slightly. On the afternoon of 13 November, the researcher noticed an island by the name of Sandy Island on the maps, but though it was included on some, it was absent on others. It was unequivocally there both on the captain's meteorological charts and in the *Times Atlas of the World*, a standard reference work that is continually updated by a team of around 50 cartographers. Yet other navigational charts clearly indicated the ocean in this sector to be between 1,300 and 1,400 metres deep. Which were correct? Certainly, it would be something of a geological miracle if the island turned out to be perched, as it were, on top of a steep pinnacle of rock rising up from the ocean floor.

On 15 November, the *Southern Surveyor* was nearing the coordinates of Sandy Island. This was when all the scientists aboard were told to scan the sea from the ship's bows, since the island might potentially be submerged just a few metres beneath the surface. The ship could be under threat from hard, jagged limestone reefs of which there were several in the eastern Coral Sea, such as those surrounding the Chesterfield Islands, an uninhabited archipelago that lay in the territorial waters of French New Caledonia. This archipelago comprises a dozen islands and hundreds of reefs covering an area measuring 70 by 120 kilometres, though all told, the islands make up no more than 10 square kilometres of dry land between them.

Captain Stein was fearful of making any detours. In all likelihood, although a number of the reefs, rocks and islands included on maps of the Western Pacific did not in fact exist, most such features were situated in the sea area east of New Zealand: for instance, the Wachusett reef, Ernest Legouvé Rock, Jupiter Reef and Maria Theresa Reef (see p. 94). So long as their existence had not been disproved beyond all doubt, they continued to be shown on maps and charts for safety's sake.

By now, the *Southern Surveyor* had reached the coordinates of Sandy Island. The scientists followed on a screen as the vessel passed through the black pixellated area shown on Google Earth. Some giggled, while others grinned at the idea that they'd proven it to be a chimera. One even suggested that they'd changed the world. A little bit, anyhow... a correction to existing maps.

On 21 November 2012, the *Southern Surveyor* returned safely to port at Brisbane. Shortly afterwards, Seton told Australian reporters about their non-discovery in the eastern Coral Sea. The news spread round the world, creating as much of a stir as if new land had been sighted.

It took a few weeks before it emerged that Sandy Island must already have been known not to exist for quite some time. In 2000, amateur – or 'ham' – radio enthusiasts had sailed to the Chesterfield Islands, which lie only about 100 kilometres away from Sandy Island. They wanted to set a world record by broadcasting from the most remote island in the world. Just by chance, they had spotted Sandy Island on a map; it seemed to be the perfect place for their test. However, they sought in vain for it and mentioned this in the report of their expedition. Even so, the cartographic 'by-catch' of their journey went unnoticed.

In November 2012, Google removed the island from its maps, but the mystery remained: who had put Sandy Island on the map in the first place, and how had this information come to be included in reputable atlases? The phantom island lies in French territorial waters, but France itself does not list the island as an official territory, and it was expunged many years earlier from French maritime charts.

Nonetheless, from 2000 onwards, the island appeared on Australian navigational charts. One source for these is the mapping data produced by the American Central Intelligence Agency (CIA). While one expert has mooted some fantastic conspiracy theory involving secret atomic tests, another thinks it more likely to be the result of an absurd error. The island, he believes, may have come into existence when old maps were in the process of being digitised: a fly allegedly got squashed between the map and the scanner (which explained why the island looked like a black hole).

The mystery of Sandy Island was finally solved in summer 2013, by one Shaun Higgins. At the time, Higgins was working as a librarian at Auckland War Memorial Museum in New Zealand. In the archives there, he came across an old record: the first appearance of Sandy Island was on a British Admiralty map of 1908. It was shown there as a dotted, cigar-shaped piece of land, the dots indicating that the cartographers were unsure of its existence. In addition, someone had made the following note in the margin of the map: 'Caution is necessary while navigating among the low-lying islands of the Pacific Ocean. The general details have been collated from the voyages of various navigators extending over a long series of years. The relative position of many dangers may therefore not be exactly given, and it is possible that there are still some undiscovered islands.' No more precise information was given.

When Higgins published his discovery on the museum's blog, though, some further details did emerge. A reader wrote to him about an entry in the Australia Directory of 1879 in which the captain of the whaling ship *Velocity* passed on two hydrographic discoveries he had made in the eastern Coral Sea: he reported seeing 'great surging billows' and 'sandy islands' running from north to south. Presumably, the Captain was concerned to warn other sailors about a dangerous stretch of ocean which he himself did not venture to inspect at closer quarters.

Perhaps the captain of the *Velocity* also thought he'd sighted an island that had been discovered less than 100 years previously by the French seafarer Antoine Bruni d'Entrecasteaux. Between 28 June and 1 July 1792, this explorer sighted a number of islands in the eastern Coral Sea, one of which he named 'Île de Sable' ('Isle of Sand'). This is identified nowadays as being one of the small islands off the northwestern tip of New Caledonia. If that were the case, then it would mean that the captain of the *Velocity* had miscalculated his position by several hundred kilometres.

SAXEMBERG
SOUTH ATLANTIC OCEAN

[SAXEMBURGH]

Position 30° 45' South, 19° 40' West
Size 19 kilometres long, 4 kilometres wide
Sightings John Lindestz Lindeman (1670),
Captain Long (1801), Captain J. O. Head (1816)
Maps uncertain

In the autumn of 1801, Captain Matthew Flinders sailed to the Cape of Good Hope. His logbook entry for Tuesday 29 September begins: 'The trade wind having again arisen from east-south-east, we were enabled to make between eighty and ninety miles a day.' Eventually, the wind veered from northeast to west, so that on this day, Flinders and his crew found themselves just 6 degrees west of the position customarily assigned to the island of Saxemberg, 'an island which has been frequently sought by the *East-India*, and other ships, in the place which it still occupies in the charts.' Yet these vessels had invariably failed to find the island. Flinders surmised that it must probably lie a few degrees farther east than marked on the maps. Sensing that he would be neglecting his duty if he didn't conduct a search for the island, Flinders steered due east to try to find it.

The first sighting of the island of Saxemberg was by the Dutch seafarer John Lindestz Lindeman in 1670. He determined its position as being 30° 45' South latitude and 19° 40' West longitude. He also made a sketch, which shows the island as being predominantly flat, but with a steep mountain rising at its centre. Lindeman is thought to have named the island after a small town in northern Germany.

On Wednesday 30 September, Flinders spotted an unusual number of pintado and sooty petrels and brown birds that he thought were a kind of sea swallow. These had a white belly and were the shape and size of a woodcock. That evening, the lookout on the masthead and other sailors on deck reported seeing a turtle. These might all be signs of land, and Flinders hoped that the elusive island of Saxemberg would soon appear.

Finally, on Thursday 1 October, Flinders determined his coordinates as 30° 34' South and 20° 28' West. He ordered the ship to steer east-southeast, a course that should have taken them almost straight to Saxemberg. In the event, their course passed a few miles south of the given coordinates, 'though sufficiently near for us to be satisfied of the non-existence of the island in the place assigned to it, if that could any longer admit of a doubt.'

Ten years later, news reached Flinders of a sailor who claimed to have recently sighted Saxemberg. One Mr Long, captain of the sloop *Columbus*, was sailing from Brazil to the Cape. On 22 September 1809, Long wrote in his logbook: 'At five p.m., saw the island of Saxonburgh [sic], bearing E. S. E., first about 41 leagues distant: clear weather. Steered for the said island, and found it to be in the latitude of 30° 18' south, longitude 28° 20' west, or thereabout.' He had approached the island, which measured about 4 leagues in length and 2.5 miles wide. At its northwestern tip there stood a high bluff, together with trees and a sandy beach.

However sceptical he may originally have been, Flinders was now convinced that Saxemberg really did exist. No one should be surprised, he commented, that he had missed the island; its position had been so imprecisely marked on charts that, on 28 September 1801, he had been a good 80 miles from the position where Long had sighted the island.

In the meantime, an American captain by the name of Galloway, master of the vessel *Fanny*, had also seen Saxemberg. Lying some 55 kilometres from his course, it stayed in view for six hours. From its centre, just as Lindeman described, there rose a steep mountain.

The existence of Saxemberg was later confirmed once more, this time by Captain J. O. Head of the *True Briton*. 'Eight o'clock, fresh breeze from the northwest and dark, overcast weather; we saw what we took to be an island,' he wrote on 9 March 1816. At its southern end was a high peak, he continued, which dropped steeply away on its northern face. Again, he kept the island in sight for a full six hours. Later, as rain set in, they lost sight of it. Nonetheless, they concluded that it had to be 'Saxemburgh.'

Lindeman's and Head's accounts are identical, as are the coordinates they cited. Yet no one has set eyes on the island since.

PALUDES NILI

30°

40°

50°

TERRA AUSTRALIS INCOGNITA

TERRA AUSTRALIS INCOGNITA
SOUTHERN OCEAN

AMERICA

Position southern hemisphere

Size larger than Asia

Sightings **Amerigo Vespucci** (1503/04), Pedro Fernández de Quirós (1605),
Jean-Baptiste Charles Bouvet de Lozier (1739)

Maps Johannes Schöner (1515)

300°

290°   280°   270°   260°   250°

They hunted with bows and arrows, killing lions, leopards and beavers whose pelts they removed in order to protect themselves from the fierce cold and wind. They used stone axes and planted curious seeds that were as large as beans; the fruits of the mature plants were as hot as chilli peppers. The grasslands in this part of the world were inhabited by large flightless birds with furry feet. Vast forests covered much of the land, and towering over them were mighty glaciers. The mountains were home to people who mined gold, silver and copper. Because there was no iron, the warriors wore armour made of gold. 'People in this region generally live to the age of 140,' wrote the Nuremberg pastor and geographer Johannes Schöner in 1515, adding that the king of Portugal was at that very time sending explorers to the continent.

The land mass in question first appeared on Schöner's globe of 1515. It was located at the South Pole and was shown as a large, circular continent, with a polar sea at its centre. Rivers crisscrossed the landscape, and there were extensive bogs and two lakes called Laco int Montaras and Laco Palus. For Schöner, this land in the far south constituted its own continent, and so he printed its name in capitals: BRASILE REGIO. He had gleaned his knowledge about it, he said, from the *Copia der Newen Zeytung aus Presillg Landt* – a copy of the *New Journal from Brazil*, which must have appeared the previous year. Schöner may also have gleaned some further details from the writings of the explorer Amerigo Vespucci, who claimed to have sailed 20 miles along the coast of the southern continent.

Even in ancient times, there had been much speculation about a southern continent. In around AD 150, the polymath Ptolemy stated that this continent bordered on the Indian Ocean to the south and that it was connected with Africa. To ensure that the Earth did not become imbalanced, all continents had to be distributed evenly across the surface of the planet. The continent was there, therefore, to serve as a counterweight to the great landmasses of the north, he claimed. In his

Geographike Hyphegesis (usually referred to as *Ptolemy's Geography*), he wrote about this 'Terra Australis,' setting forth his explanation in logical terms: 'The part of the world inhabited by us is connected in the east to an unknown land, which borders on the eastern rivers of Greater Asia, and in the south likewise to an unknown land, which surrounds the Indian Ocean.' Ptolemy was unequivocally indicating the existence of another continent south of the Indian Ocean.

In the Middle Ages, Ptolemy's ideas were adopted by Christian thinkers: since God's creation was perfect, it followed that all the parts of the Earth were in a celestial symmetry. And so, the fifth continent appeared thenceforth on many maps of the world. By the late 16th century, it was shown as occupying a large portion of the south and was identified as Terra Australis Incognita, 'the unknown land in the South.'

In 1567, while exploring the Pacific, the Spanish navigator Alvaro de Mendaña de Neira thought Melanesia might be the first outpost of the southern continent. Later, the Portuguese adventurer Pedro Fernández de Quirós came to believe that Terra Australis extended from New Guinea as far as South America and was as large as Europe and Asia combined. In 1605, he founded a missionary station on Espiritu Santo, the largest island in the Vanuatu archipelago. He thought it was an outlying island of the southern continent and regarded it as his mission to convert the 'savages' to Christianity. Before long, this missionary work began to be conducted through violent coercion.

Terra Australis was still being shown on maps as late as the 18th century. When Jean-Baptiste Charles Bouvet de Lozier discovered Bouvet Island (see p. 30) in the South Atlantic in 1739, he hoped that it might represent a jumping-off point from which to explore the unknown continent.

After the British achieved mastery of the world's oceans during the Seven Years' War (1756–63), Captain James Cook was charged with the task of finding the southern continent. 'There is reason to imagine that a Continent or Land of great extent, may be found to the South-ward of the Tract lately made by Capt. Wallis in His Majesty's Ship the *Dolphin*,' Cook noted before embarking on his first voyage to the South Pacific in 1768. Cook traversed vast areas of the Pacific during his two famous voyages to the region. In 1775, at the end of his second voyage, Cook resignedly concluded that he had at least put 'a final end [...] to the searching after a Southern Continent, which has at times ingrossed the attention of some of the Maritime Powers for near two Centuries past and the Geographers of all ages.'

GREENLAND

Alba

Grimle

Tulios
Anafjord

THULE

Griflada

FRISLAND

THULE · ATLANTIC OCEAN

[TILE, TULL, TYLE]

Position **63rd parallel north**
Size **uncertain**
Sightings **c.330 BC**
Maps *Carta Marina* **(1539)**

N ever before had northern Europe been depicted so precisely and accurately: in 1539, the Swedish priest Olaus Magnus published his *Carta Marina*, a 'sea chart and description of the Northern lands and their wonders.' Magnus had spent 12 years working on this masterpiece. From the Barents Sea in the North via Greenland in the West and as far as Russia in the East, it presented Europeans with an extraordinarily clear and colourful picture of the north of their continent. Little pictures of galleons indicated fishing grounds, trade routes or mighty whirlpools. The seas were full of magnificent and bizarre creatures frolicking about, including sea pigs, giant lobsters and poisonous snakes. Norway was shown with its heavily indented coastline of fjords, and between Scotland and Iceland was a mysterious island called 'Tile,' complete with settlements, a castle, forests and meadows. Off the southern coast of Tile, we can see a whale (labelled Balena) under attack by a killer whale (Orcha).

Magnus's map was based on an old compendium of geographical knowledge that had been amassed some 1,400 years before by the Graeco-Roman polymath Ptolemy. By Ptolemy's time, the Roman Empire had expanded to almost incalculable proportions, and so he began collating the coordinates of some 7,000 Roman settlements in around AD 150. His data came predominantly from military surveying units of the Roman army and the forces of Alexander the Great; even then, using the position of the sun, it was possible to work out a site's coordinates to within 10 kilometres. Ptolemy listed them in his gazetteer *Geographike Hyphegesis*. He determined the centre of the island of 'Thule' as being at the latitude of 63° North and relied on accounts which claimed that Scythian peoples still lived north of Thule. He also insisted that Roman military expeditions had sighted the island when they sailed around the British Isles. In fact, it may well be the case that Ptolemy's Thule was in fact one of the Shetland Islands.

Even in antiquity, though, Thule must have been a place of legend. The earliest mention of it dates back to a travel report by the Greek astronomer Pytheas. As early as 330 BC, he undertook a research expedition to the far north of Europe. From his hometown of Massalia, the site of the modern French port of Marseilles, he sailed to the British Isles, then travelled over to Ireland aboard an ox-hide boat (currach), and it is also likely that he set foot on Orkney and Shetland. On his journey, Pytheas managed to make some extraordinarily accurate geographical measurements, investigate the question of the inclination of the Earth's axis and finally make the observation that the tides are dependent upon the phases of the moon. But this brilliant natural historian felt the urge to venture even farther out to sea. A long way from the British Isles, Pytheas discovered a place at the ends of the known world, to which he gave the name 'Ultima Thule.'

Tragically, Pytheas's account of his travels, *Peri tou Okeanou* (*On the Ocean*), has been lost. Only fragments of it were digested in the works of later authors, such as Strabo's *Geography*, Pliny the Elder's *Natural History* and the *Isagoge* of Geminus, which contains the only verbatim quotation from Pytheas: 'In these climes, the nights were very short.'

According to ancient natural scientists, Thule was a six-day sea journey somewhere north of Britain. Though this sounds to us like a very rough approximation, it might in fact be a very precise indication of distance. A day's voyage in the Middle Ages is reckoned to equate to 156.5 kilometres. Six times this figure would give a distance of some 940 kilometres, leaving aside the strength of the wind.

Accordingly, Pytheas could have reached Iceland from the British Isles in that time. One report from antiquity claims that the nights in Thule lasted two to three hours. And in fact, during the summer solstice, it is dark for only three hours in the south of Iceland, while in the north the nights are just two hours long. Some ancient sources also spoke of a 'frozen sea' spreading out just another day's journey on from Thule, which must surely mean huge amounts of drift ice. That would also point to Iceland as being Thule.

Yet Pytheas also recounted meeting people who were growing grain and harvesting honey – Iceland, however, was unsettled at the time he was writing. Plus, in none of the ancient sources that refer to his journey is there a single mention of geysers and volcanoes, Iceland's most characteristic features then as now.

If Pytheas had not sailed due north of Britain, though, but had taken a northeasterly course instead, he would have come to the coast of Norway. At that time, there were communities on the island of Smøla and along the Trondheim Fjord who lived in permanent settlements and practised settled agriculture. Indeed, deep strata of fertile clay soils are found along the length of this fjord, while the warm North Atlantic Current makes for a mild, damp climate.

As on Iceland, summer days on the Trondheim Fjord and Smøla are very long. Pytheas would only have had to sail north along the Norwegian coast for another few kilometres to find a location where the nights were just three hours long. He may even have been the very first southern European to see the midnight sun.

Yet no subsequent ancient author reports that Pytheas saw a fjord; the only bodies of water mentioned are rivers. But even more suspect is the absence at that latitude in Norway of the 'curdled sea' to which Pytheas refers: neither today nor at the time when Pytheas made his journey has there ever been any record of icebergs drifting into the Atlantic past Smøla. Perhaps the image of the 'curdled sea' was, as is so often the case in literature, merely an elegant turn of phrase, designed to make the story sound more colourful and imaginative in the same way that the cartographer Olaus Magnus surely did not take the existence of sea monsters and giant crustaceans at face value.

TUANAKI · PACIFIC OCEAN

[TUANAHE, ULTIMATELY ALSO HAYMET ROCKS]

Position 27° 11' South, 160° 13' West

Size uncertain

Sightings 1841, 1863

Maps uncertain

In 1863, Captain J. E. Haymet was sailing with his schooner *Will Watch* from New Zealand to the Cook Islands. All of a sudden, out on the open ocean, the ship rammed a rock. As Haymet was inspecting the damaged hull of his vessel, he noticed another rock sticking out of the sea farther to the south. Furthermore, the sea was barely two metres deep at this point. He determined the coordinates of these shallows as 27° 11' South, 160° 13' West. Before long, seafarers and scientists were puzzling over whether the rocks that Haymet encountered so violently – henceforth dubbed the Haymet Rocks – were a remnant of the legendary island of Tuanaki.

The indigenous inhabitants of the Cook Islands had long told tales of Tuanaki; it was said to consist of three low-lying islands shielded by a reef. Getting there, apparently, meant sailing for two days by canoe in a southwesterly direction from Rarotonga.

In 1843, Reverend William Gill set off with a Cook Island native as his guide in search of Tuanaki. En route, they stopped over on the island of Aitutaki, where a dysentery epidemic was raging. It had already claimed the lives of 30 people. There, they made the acquaintance of a man called Soma, who told them about Tuanaki. He claimed to have visited the island just two years previously, rowing over to it with the captain of a large ship that had anchored offshore. On landing, the captain ordered him to strike out in search of natives, armed with a sword. Eventually, he found himself outside the house of the Ariki, the leader of the island.

From inside, the Ariki called out: 'Where have you come from? Are you from Araura?' Soma entered the building. Inside, he found a group of men sitting down, who asked him where the captain was. When they assured him that no stranger need be afraid of them, since their skills lay in dancing rather than fighting, Soma went back to fetch the captain. He took presents with him – including an axe and a hat – which he handed over in the Ariki's house. That evening, the island-ers sent a boat laden with chickens, pigs, yams, bananas, taro and coconuts to the newcomers' ship. Soma and the captain had stayed on Tuanaki for six days.

Reverend Gill listened to the story in silence, and when it was over, he was keen to learn more about the people on Tuanaki. 'They're just like us,' Soma explained, 'they heed the authority of the Ariki and have to pay their tributes to him in the form of food.' They apparently spoke the same dialect as the inhabitants of Aitutaki and wore the same kind of ponchos. The island was no more than a night's sail away, but he himself had no intention of going there now, not even in return for payment. His sister was dying of dysentery, he told Gill, and a second sister had already succumbed to the disease.

So Reverend Gill abandoned his plan for the time being. The fol-lowing year, rumour had it that Tuanaki had sunk during a volcanic eruption like Atlantis (see p. 16). Only a handful of survivors had been able to save themselves. The Haymet Rocks, which were said to jut out of the water like two lonely towers, may well have been a remnant of the island. But no one has ever managed to find them since.

WILLOUGHBY'S LAND
ARCTIC OCEAN

Position 72° North

Size uncertain

Sightings 1553

Maps Petrus Plancius (1594)

As the ice began to thaw in the spring of 1554, the Pomor fishermen of northwestern Russia set off for their remote fishing grounds in the Barents Sea. They had never encountered any foreigners there before, but now, lying at anchor off the estuary of the Varzina River, they found two ghostly ships that were much larger than their own. There was no smoke rising from their galleys, and not a soul was to be seen on deck. The fishermen hailed the vessels but received no reply; not a sound could be heard. They climbed on board, broke down the doors and recoiled in horror at the sight that met their eyes: bunk after bunk of soldiers, sailors and merchants, all frozen stiff.

The fishermen found a notebook on one of the ships, which they handed over to the governor of the region. It was the property of the British merchant adventurer Sir Hugh Willoughby, who recounted in its pages the drama that had unfolded on board the *Bona Esperanza* and the *Bona Confidentia*.

Almost a year before, in 1553, Willoughby set sail from London with three ships. Like many geographers, he believed in the existence of Northwest Passage, a sea route past the North Pole to the Far East. Accordingly, he had made extravagant promises to his patrons of undiscovered regions, new realms and, above all, a shorter trade route to China. As the ships left the River Thames, hundreds of people stood waving at the quaysides, cannons roared and, from a tower, the boy king Edward VI hailed the flotilla. Although the *Bona Esperanza*, the *Edward Bonaventura* and the *Bona Confidentia* were equipped for the winter, Willoughby and his men were keen to get to their destination well before.

Willoughby was an experienced soldier who had fought in campaigns on the Scottish border, yet he knew very little about maritime matters; at sea, his captains would be responsible. They had ordered prayer sessions to be held on board every morning, banned games of dice and warned the sailors to resist the allure of mermaids. The fleet spent the first few weeks sailing to Norway and following its coast north. At the beginning of August, they were off the Lofoten Islands when a violent storm blew up and the ships became separated. Alone, the *Edward Bonaventura* made for the port of Vardøhus on the small island of Vardøya off the far northeastern coast of Norway to await the arrival of the other ships – a plan agreed beforehand for such emergencies.

After a week of waiting, the ship continued its onward journey alone. Captain Richard Chancellor sailed past the Kola Peninsula to the White Sea, then traversed unknown waters before finally reaching a harbour in St Nicholas Bay near to the modern city of Severodvinsk. From there, Chancellor and some of his crew were escorted overland to Moscow and warmly received in the Kremlin by Tsar Ivan the Terrible. Together, they celebrated the newly discovered trade route between England and Russia.

Meanwhile, the *Bona Esperanza* and the *Bona Confidentia* had anchored in a rocky bay on the Kola Peninsula, around 150 kilometres east of modern Murmansk. They had only reached the agreed rendezvous point at Vardøhus after Chancellor had already left. They waited for several days, and then lost even more time on their onward journey. 'On the 14th day [of August], early in the morning we sighted land. We let down our ship's boat in order to find out what manner of land this might be, but were unable to make it to shore,' Willoughby noted in his journal. It is unclear from his notes exactly why they could not make land – perhaps the water was too shallow there or choked with kelp. In any event, they could not see any signs of people or human habitation. The island they saw 'was located in the latitude of 72°,' and hence somewhere north of Norway.

Willoughby and his crew of 62 were the first Europeans to overwinter in the Arctic Circle. They saw bears, foxes, herds of reindeer and huge shoals of fish. When the weather grew colder, reconnaissance parties were despatched in all directions to look for settlements, but to no avail. Willoughby's journal ends with their return. Ultimately, however, it was the intense cold that sealed the men's fate: because they were heating the ships by burning coal and had plugged every gap to prevent draughts, it is thought that they all died of carbon monoxide poisoning.

Their frozen bodies were only found by the Russian fishermen in May of the following year. The tragedy shocked England. The island that Willoughby reported sighting was named in his honour, even though no one knew precisely where it was.

Four decades after the catastrophe, the Dutch cartographer Petrus Plancius included Willoughby Island on his 1594 map of the North Polar region. He placed it in the Barents Sea, while at the same time noting that he doubted its existence and that there was only one reason for including it – he did not want anyone to be able to accuse him of drawing an incomplete map.

When the explorer Henry Hudson failed to find the island in 1610, many commentators in England reacted defiantly by claiming that it must have been Bear Island, or even Spitsbergen, that Willoughby discovered. The reputation of a national hero had to be upheld at all costs.

AUTHOR'S NOTES

A note on the maps

All the maps illustrating the phantom islands were prepared specially for this book and are based in each case on historical models. A kaleidoscope of 600 years of mapping history, from all the great names in cartography, is assembled here. This also explains why many unfamiliar outlines of islands appear and why the way in which they relate to familiar areas of land sometimes appears absurd.

Readers might also be perplexed by the degrees of longitude shown, given that they do not always correspond to our modern segmentation of the world. The reason for this is the reform of longitudinal measurements that was agreed upon at the International Meridian Conference held in Washington, D.C. in 1884.

So, just like the phantom islands themselves, although the maps in this book often do not bear much resemblance to reality, they do reflect all the more accurately the sheer inventiveness of the individuals who 'discovered' the lands and those who mapped them in their respective eras.

A note on my research

This small compendium of phantom islands makes no claim to academic rigour, nor does it pretend to be at all comprehensive. The source material proved to be tricky: to date, there is only a very limited body of secondary literature available; this includes the works by Donald Johnson, Henry Stommel and Raymond H. Ramsay cited in the following bibliography. But even these works are primarily concerned with a handful of islands in the Atlantic. If my research had been forced to rely solely on works in municipal and university libraries, then this book would never have seen the light of day. Fortunately, quite a number of centuries-old primary sources – or at the very least extracts from them – are now available on the internet. In addition, virtual specialist libraries hold many logbooks of explorers and seafarers, or even academic treatises containing excerpts from logbooks. Even so, it was not possible in every case to retrace exactly where and when the original works in question had first been published. And all too frequently, the treatises did not cite the sources for the passages they quoted. Therefore, the list of sources that follows only presents a selection of works by those authors who appear prominently in one entry or another.

BIBLIOGRAPHY

ANTILIA

Paolo dal Pozzo Toscanelli: Letter to Fernando Martinez (25 June 1474); in McKew Parr Collection: *Magellan and the Age of Discovery* (presented to Brandeis University in 1961)

ATLANTIS

Plato: *Critias* and *Timaeus* (4th century BC)
Athanasius Kircher: *Mundus Subterraneus* (1664–1678)

AURORA ISLANDS

Amerigo Vespucci: *Lettera* (1505)
James Weddell: *Voyage towards the South Pole* (Longman, Hurst, Rees, Orme, Brown and Green, London, 1825); abstract in Henry Stommel: *Lost Islands* (University of British Columbia Press, Vancouver, 1984)
Edgar Allan Poe: *The Narrative of Arthur Gordon Pym of Nantucket* (Penguin Books, London, 2008)

BALTIA

Pytheas of Massalia: *Peri tou Okeanou* (4th century BC)
Diodorus Siculus: *Bibliotheca historica* (1st century BC)
Pliny the Elder: *Naturalis Historia* (c. 77)
Works quoted in August Friedrich Pauly: *Real-Encyclopädie der class. Alterthumswissenschaft in alphabetischer Ordnung: Vol. 3* (Metzler, Stuttgart, 1992)

BERMEJA

Alonso de Chaves: *Espejo de Navegantes* (1536); quoted after Carlos Contreras Servín: 'La cartografía como testimonio de la identidad territorial de las culturas prehispánicas' (*Boletín del Sistema Nacional de Información Estadística y Geográfica*, Vol. 2, No. 3, 2009)

BOUVET GROUP

Carl Chun: *Aus den Tiefen des Weltmeeres* (G. Fischer, Jena, 1903)

BUSS

Thomas Wiars' report in Richard Hakluyt: *The Principal Navigations, Voyages, Traffiques and Discoveries of the English Nation* (J. MacLehose and Sons, Glasgow, 1903)

Donald Johnson: *Fata Morgana der Meere* (Diana Verlag, Munich, 1999)

BYERS AND MORRELL ISLANDS

Benjamin Morrell: *A Narrative of Four Voyages* (J. & J. Harper, New York, 1832); quoted in Henry Stommel: *Lost Islands* (University of British Columbia Press, Vancouver, 1984)

CALIFORNIA

Garci Rodríguez de Montalvo: *The Exploits of Esplandián* (1510)

Francisco Preciado: 'Relacion de los descubrimientos, hechos por Don Francisco de Ulloa en un viage por la Mar del Morte, en el navio Santa Agueda' 1556; in English in James Burney: *A Chronological History of the Discoveries in the South Sea or Pacific Ocean* (Cambridge University Press, Cambridge, 2010)

CROCKER LAND
Donald Baxter MacMillan: 'In search of a new land' (*Harper's Magazine*, October/November 1915)
idem: *Four Years in the White North* (Harper & Brothers, New York and London, 1918)

FRISLAND
Nicolò Zeno the Younger: *De I Commentarii del Viaggo* (1558); quoted in Donald S. Johnson: *Fata Morgana der Meere* (Diana Verlag, Zurich, 1994)

HARMSWORTH ISLAND
Arthur Koestler: *Arrow in the Blue* (Vintage Publishing, London, 2005)
Lincoln Ellsworth and Edward H. Smith: 'Report of the Preliminary Results of the Aeroarctic Expedition with Graf Zeppelin (1931)' (*Geographical Review*, Vol. 22, No. 1, January 1932, pp. 61–82)
Frederick George Jackson: *A Thousand Days in the Arctic* (Harper & Brothers, New York and London, 1899)

JUAN DE LISBOA
Maurice Benyowsky: *Memoirs and Travels of Mauritius Augustus Count de Benyowsky* (P. Wogan, Dublin 1790)
Elli Narewska, Susan Gentles, Mariam Yamin: 'April fool – San Serriffe: teaching resource of the month from the GNM Archive, April 2012' (*The Guardian*, 27 March 2012)

KANTIA

Volkmar Billig: *Inseln. Geschichte einer Faszination* (Matthes & Seitz, Berlin, 2010)

Axel Bojanowski: 'Ein Traum von einer Insel' (*Süddeutsche Zeitung*, 17 May 2010)

Axel Bojanowski: 'Kartenmysterium vor Australien' (*Spiegel Online*, 22 November 2012)

Axel Bojanowski: *Nach zwei Tagen Regen folgt Montag: Und andere rätselhafte Phänomene des Planeten Erde* (DVA, Munich, 2012)

Rainer Godel and Gideon Stiening (ed.): 'Klopffechtereien – Missverständnisse – Widersprüche? Methodische und methodologische Perspektiven auf die Kant-Forster-Kontroverse' (*Laboratorium Aufklärung*, Vol. 10, Wilhelm Fink Verlag, 2011)

Sebastian Herrmann: *Die fliegende Katze: 1000 Kuriositäten aus dem Alltag* (Knaur, Munich, 2010)

Samuel Herzog: 'Die Wilden scheinen wohl gesonnen – Unterwegs in einer fiktionalen Meereslandschaft' (*Neue Zürcher Zeitung*, 22 May 2004)

Ulli Kulke: 'Wie Inseln plötzlich von den Karten verschwinden' (*Die Welt, Hamburger Abendblatt* and *Berliner Morgenpost*, 7 December 2012)

Stefan Nink: 'Meer in Sicht! Island Fantasies' (*Lufthansa Magazin*, August 2012)

KEENAN LAND

Marcus Baker: 'An Undiscovered Island off the Northern Coast of Alaska' (*National Geographic Magazine 5*, 1894)

KOREA

Jan Huyghen van Linschoten: *Reys-gheshift vande navigatien der Portugaloysers in Orienten* (1595) and *Itinerario, voyage, ofte Schipvaert van Jan Huygen van Linschoten naer Oost ofte Portugaels Indien* (1595); quoted in John R. Short: *Korea: A Cartographic History* (University of Chicago Press, Chicago, 2012)

Henny G. L. Savenije: 'Korea in Western Cartography' (*Korean Culture*, Vol. 21, No. 1, 2000)

MARIA THERESA REEF
Jules Verne: *Les Enfants du capitaine Grant* (Hetzel, Paris, 1868)
Bernhard Krauth: research on Andreas Fehrmann's website: www.j-verne.de (date of access: June 2016)

NEW SOUTH GREENLAND
Benjamin Morrell: *A Narrative of Four Voyages* (J. & J. Harper, New York, 1832)
Sir Ernest Shackleton: *South: The Endurance Expedition* (Signet, New York, 1999)
Wilhelm Filchner, Alfred Kling, Erich Przybyllok: *Zum sechsten Erdteil – Die Zweite Deutsche Südpolar-Expedition* (Ullstein Verlag, Berlin, 1922)

PEPYS ISLAND
William Hacke: *Collection of Original Voyages* (1699)

PHÉLIPEAUX AND PONTCHARTRAIN
Treaty of Paris (3 September 1783)
J.P.D. Dunbabin: 'Motives for Mapping the Great Lakes: Upper Canada, 1782–1827' (*Michigan Historical Review*, Vol. 31, No. 1, Spring 2005, pp. 1–43)

RUPES NIGRA

Gerardus Mercator: Letter to John Dee (20 April 1577); quoted after *Imago Mundi*, Vol. 13, Imago Mundi, Lrd. (1956)

Anonymous: *Inventio Fortunata* (c. 1364); see also Chet Van Duzer: 'The Mythic Geography of the Northern Polar Regions: Inventio fortunata and Buddhist Cosmology' (*Culturas Populares*. *Revista Electrónica* 2, May–August 2006)

Jacobus Cnoyen of Herzogenbusch: *Res gestae Arturi britanni*

Jonathan Swift: *Gulliver's Travels* (Benjamin Motte, London, 1726)

SAINT BRENDAN'S ISLANDS

Anonymous: *Navigatio Sancti Brendani* (c. 570)

Honorius Augustodunensis, *Imago Mundi* (c. 1100)

Gervase of Tilbury, *Otia Imperialia* (early 13th century)

José de Viera y Clavijo: *Noticias* (La Imprenta de Blas Román, Madrid, 1772)

SANDY ISLAND

Australia Directory Volume 2; 3rd Edition (1879)

SAXEMBERG

Matthew Flinders: *A Voyage to Terra Australis* (G. & W. Nicol, London, 1814)

TERRA AUSTRALIS INCOGNITA

Claudius Ptolemy: *Geographike Hyphegesis* (c. 150)

Johannes Schöner: *Luculentissima* (1515); quoted after Frank Berger (ed.): *Der Erdglobus des Johannes Schöner von 1515* (Henrich Editionen, Historisches Museum Frankfurt, 2013)

THULE

Pytheas of Massalia: *On the Ocean* (4th century BC)

Geminus of Rhodes: *Isagoge*

Quoted in: Christian Marx: 'Lokalisierung von Pytheas' und Ptolemaios' Thule'. (*zfv – Zeitschrift für Geodäsie, Geoinformation und Landmanagement*, Vol. 139, June 2014, pp. 197–203)

TUANAKI

Quoted after Henry Stommel: *Lost Islands* (University of British Columbia Press, Vancouver, 1984)

WILLOUGHBY'S LAND

Willoughby's notes in Richard Hakluyt: *Principal Navigations, Vol. 2* (J. MacLehose and sons, Glasgow, 1903)

John Pinkerton: *Voyages and Travels in all Parts of the World* (Longman, Hurst, Rees, Orme and Brown, London, 1812)

Eleanora C. Gordon: ' The Fate of Sir Hugh Willoughby and His Companions: A New Conjecture' (*The Geographical Journal*, Vol. 152, No. 2, July 1986, pp. 243–247)